Swallowed Up:
Loving Others Without Losing Yourself

by Angie Shea

© 2016 Angie Shea

Published by WI Publish, a Division of Women Ignite International.

All rights reserved. No part of this publication may be reproduced, stored in a retrieval system, or transmitted in any form by any means—for example, electronic, photocopy, recording—without the prior written permission of the publisher. The only exception is brief quotations in printed reviews.

The stories contained in this book are true, based on the individual views of the author.

www.AngieShea.com

Table of Contents

Dedication	5
Acknowledgements	7
Foreword	9
Introduction	11
Chapter 1	17
Chapter 2	25
Chapter 3	51
Chapter 4	57
Chapter 5	67
Chapter 6	83
Chapter 7	103
Chapter 8	125
Chapter 9	139
Chapter 10	159
Chapter 11	173
Chapter 12	187
About Angie Shea	190
Stay Connected	191

Swallowed Up

Dedication

This book is lovingly dedicated to my amazing adult children, Jared Shea and Kaylee (Shea) Spaeth, who are two of the best human beings I know. Thank you for loving me and making me the most blessed mother in the world.

Acknowledgements

I am truly grateful to so many who have inspired me to continue the journey of teaching classes and ultimately completing this book. Your bravery and dedication to implement these principles into your lives, no matter the cost, has been a testimony and confirmation of this great "work" that I feel called to do.

I want to say thank you to my dear friend and boundaries mentor, Wanda Hodges, who continues to pour into my life her amazing wisdom and unconditional love. Your encouragement and guidance have truly changed my life forever, and I am honored to continue to carry the torch and mentor others on their boundaries journey so that your legacy and calling lives on.

I owe a debt of gratitude to Norm Stueckle, my beloved friend, mentor and counselor who could see things in me before I could see them in myself. It is no accident that our paths crossed during a crucial time of development for me, and I promise to use what you taught me and give you credit (occasionally).

I am incredibly blessed with the most amazing sister, Sheli Gartman, who is also my first and best friend, and who has been my biggest supporter and encourager. Without her love, support and belief in me when I didn't believe in myself, this would never have been accomplished.

I want to thank my friend Renee' Settle, who encouraged me to write my story. Thank you my friend for not letting me give up on this project.

I am grateful to WI Publish and Terilee Harrison for her support and guidance in bringing Swallowed Up to print.

There are so many who have contributed to my journey, and who continue to walk this road of life with me, and I am grateful for each one of you. How blessed I am to have so many surrounding me with love and encouragement.

I am so grateful to my amazing illustrator, Jessica Tookey, for creating the cover for this book. I am in awe of her talent, and so glad she was able to take the time to share her gift with me and everyone who reads it.

Foreword

Over the last 18 years as a Facilitator and Life Coach, I have seen what a huge detriment not being able to establish boundaries has on people's lives. I have worked with thousands of people from around the world, and lack of setting boundaries is a universal issue. Swallowed Up is a much needed work in the world today.

Angie Shea has a remarkable story of love and loss. Of living with a soul wide open, and then learning that boundaries are a key to any healthy life, and soul survival. She "stumbled" onto becoming the boundaries coach and expert that she is today, if you believe in accidents that big. But in doing her own courageous work of setting limits, and learning that it was the only way to have healthy, sustainable relationships that enhance your life, vs. ones that swallow you up, she unlocked a calling much bigger than herself. To know Angie is to love her. To respect her. There is no one more honest, more giving, and more about serving people, even as an introvert. But, even if you are a driver, achiever, extroverted, and accomplished in corporate America, or as an Entrepreneur, who thinks you know all about boundaries--guess again. I learned this, too. The many layers to this topic and its applications will blow away the left brained intellectual, and the artistic visionary types, and everyone in-between.

Angie brings a completely fresh take to something that personal development consultants and most therapists have known for decades; that knowing how and when and with whom to set healthy boundaries, at home and at work, will set you free to expand into your best life.

SheliG

International Speaker | CEO Women Ignite International | Team Igniter | Corporate Comedian | Author "The Ignited Entrepreneur"

Swallowed Up

Introduction

It had been another challenging year. My pastor husband and I had moved with our two small children to a small town on the Kenai Peninsula in Alaska to pastor a small church. We were excited, but there were a lot of things that would take us out of our comfort zones on a regular basis. It was very cold, and during the 8 months of winter, there were months where there was very little sunlight. We were far away from family, and it was quite expensive on our budget to make the trip home to see family very often, and it was the same for them getting up to see us.

We met so many wonderful people who were for the most part excited to have our young family there to infuse new life into the church. However, we found out quickly that these people were definitely survivalists; they had to be to thrive in this isolated and difficult culture. They were glad to have us there, but they made quite clear to us that "we were here before you came, and we will be here when you leave." In other words, we were definitely choosing into their world and way of life and not the other way around.

Then there were the common expectations that members of many churches have of the pastoral family, most of which we had learned to accept and even embrace, although it was a little stressful to be in the limelight all of the time. It was the typical "life in the fishbowl" which in all fairness was probably partially real and somewhat perceived. Regardless, I was quite happy for the most part in my role as the minister's wife, and believed I was quite good at it!

After a year of mysterious physical symptoms that caused me to be ill about one weekend out of every month, including a couple of overnight stays at the hospital; it was decided by a surgeon in Anchorage that I was having gall bladder issues and needed to have it removed. We traveled to Anchorage and had the surgery and came back within a few days for me to recover. Due to the nature of the surgery, I was told to expect 1-3 weeks of recovery time. The first week was quite rough, but after that

I began to feel better and was anxious to not be cooped up any more, so I decided I would attempt to attend church the following Sunday.

I had served in several capacities in addition to supporting my husband. I was the Coordinator and Facilitator of the Worship Team, which I also sang in. It went along with my natural gifting, and I was happy to be in charge of it. It was not a big church, about 125 people at the most, so we didn't have an overabundance of people who sang or who wanted the weekly commitment of extra practices and showing up early for services. It was quite challenging if anyone was sick or out of town, because we only had one voice to cover each part. I was having a hard time finding anyone to take my spot, so I reluctantly decided that if I laid low all week and tried not to overdo it I could go ahead and sing with the worship team that Sunday (a week after my surgery).

I vividly remember being approached by a layperson in the church (we will call her "Anna") who was in charge of another ministry that I was usually a part of. I had already decided that leading the Worship Team was probably pushing it, so I would not participate in the other activities I regularly was a part of so as to not do myself in physically. Anna approached me in the foyer of the church, and she wasn't hiding that she was frustrated. She was one of those people that had such a strong presence that you could feel her energy way before she even got close to you.

As she drew closer she made a huffing sound and very abruptly said, "We missed you in rehearsal. You are planning to participate today, aren't you?"

I was quite sure that she was aware of my recent surgery, and thought she would just be glad or surprised to see me, but obviously that wasn't the case. I replied, and said with a smile, "You know, I'm just so happy that I feel well enough to be here this morning. I really didn't feel up to leading and singing on the worship team this morning, but I couldn't find anyone to take my place, so I decided I would just push and get through it, but I'm pretty sure that's all I can do this morning."

I figured it was a reasonable explanation and waited for her body language and her energy to soften, and for her condescending tone to change to a compassionate one, but I soon realized that was not the direction this was going to go.

She huffed again, "Well, we are really short today and could use your help."

It was probably a good thing I felt the way I did that day, because as much as I wanted people to like me and approve of me, I knew that I simply couldn't do more than I was. I just didn't have it in me.

"Anna, you know I am very consistent and I am always here and participating unless I have a really good reason, and today is one of those days where I just can't do it."

I was quite relieved when she rolled her eyes and walked away. "Wow, I thought to myself, I'm glad that's over." I was also a little proud of myself that I had stood my ground, because that wasn't typical for me. I thought it was over and we would all move on. That's what I planned to do.

I was quite spent and not feeling too great after the service, but months before we had planned a church board lunch meeting for after church. I wanted to go and support my husband and at least make a showing, and so I did.

We all made our way through the potluck line and into the living room of the house we were meeting at. The board members moved into the next room while I joined the circle of spouses that had formed. I was more than surprised when Anna approached me again, and in front of 6 or 7 other people said, "I still don't understand why you couldn't have participated today." I could hardly believe what I was hearing. Did she really just say that to me? Did we not just have this conversation? It's not like I was a flake or just making up an excuse, I really shouldn't have been there at all, and she frankly didn't care. "Anna, I explained to you earlier that I was sorry that you were short-handed, but that it was all I could do just to participate in the worship team for the service". "Well," she sneered, "it's just interesting to me that you could muster up enough strength to participate in your ministry, but you couldn't find it in yourself to help with mine." The room was dead silent. It was beyond awkward. No one knew what to do or say. My face flushed. I felt suddenly hot, and I became totally unaware of everything around me. All I could see was her face, and feel the shame that she was trying to project on me. She was acting like I had done something wrong. It was like being taken back to grade school when the teacher got cross and chastised us for our behavior, except that I was an adult. And I was ill. I thought she was my friend. I was totally humiliated. I said nothing. She turned abruptly and walked away.

I'm sure this all took place within a matter of minutes, possibly seconds, but it felt like an eternity. I stood there in a daze until I realized that everyone was watching to see what I would do next. In that moment, I knew that I had to get out of there. I had already been fatigued and in pain, but now it was just magnified. "Just hold it together, Angie. Don't meltdown," I told myself. I straightened my shoulders, politely excused myself and smiled as I told everyone goodbye, but inside, something had snapped.

As soon as I was out of sight of anyone, I burst into tears. The sobs racked my body with pain. I held my surgery site and doubled over as I tried to make my way to the car and get home where I was safe. What just happened? I thought she was my friend.

On Monday morning, I promptly made an appointment with my family doctor, an amazing woman who had been through a lot with me in a short period of time. I had been struggling with the darkness, the loneliness, my physical issues, and I needed to see her. After years of struggling with clinical depression that is hereditary, I knew I couldn't mess around. I was spiraling fast, and I needed to check in with someone I trusted.

Swallowed Up

I was waiting in the exam room wondering what I would say to her. I wanted to cry. I wanted to scream. I wanted to quit everything. I knew I couldn't, but something had just snapped inside me, and I was at a loss as to what to do. When she came in, she smiled as usual and said, "Angela, what can I do for you today?" One amazing gift that I have received from my parents is the ability to find and create humor in most situations. It's been a great coping tool for me over the years. This was one of those times, so half kidding and half dead serious I said, "Well, you know how when a child is sick or injured and they can't play a sport or participate in some other activity, they have to get a doctor's note to be excused?" With a puzzled look she replied, "Yes?" I continued, "I need you to write me a note that says I'm excused from being a pastor's wife, and that it is definitely not in my best interest to live in Alaska." I'm sure for a moment she probably wanted to laugh, but she didn't, because she could see the absolute desperation on my face. She immediately pulled up a chair and sat directly in front of me. "Okay, Angela, talk to me. What is going on?" she inquired.

I told her what had happened the day before, and through tears I said, "I don't know what I'm going to do! I just know that I can't handle one more person, especially one that I thought cared about me and called me their friend, do or say anything like that to me again." She asked me a few more questions about what happened, but she mostly just listened with compassion, something I desperately needed. Anyone who has been in ministry leadership before knows it can be a very lonely place. What I needed most was a safe, neutral space to be brutally honest about what was going on inside me. After several more minutes of tears and venting, she stood up and said, "Wait right here, I'll be back." Within a minute she returned with a book in her hand that talked about how to set boundaries in your life. Boundaries? What in the world were boundaries? She told me she had read about half of the book, and that it was so good, but that I obviously needed it way worse than she did. She insisted that I take it home and read it, and then she referred me to a counselor; the first time I had ever gone to therapy in my life.

I read the book and returned it within a week. I was fascinated, perplexed, confused by all of this business about "Boundaries". It seemed so counterintuitive to what I had believed was the "right" way to do things and it definitely didn't seem like the "spiritual" perspective I had grown up with. I didn't understand how it worked, and I honestly couldn't picture myself ever implementing it into my life. Yet I knew that what I had done up until that point wasn't working, and I figured it was at least worth exploring. After all, it was written by two Christian psychologists, so it couldn't be too far off-base.

Along with counseling and reading and re-reading that book, and then the mentoring and therapy I received, years later I began eventually facilitating my own classes on the subject. I had gained the tools to set limits and take back the power that I had given away for so long, and I wanted to help others to see that they could do the same.

My hope and prayer as you read this book is that you will discover ways to have healthy relationships and most of all live life as you were meant to live it: responsible for you, doing what you can, and knowing that each night when you lay your head down that you have done everything that you need to do in order to create the life you want and influence the ones you love. Most importantly, I want you to realize that it is possible to do all of that without losing yourself, stuffing your feelings, hiding your voice, and living the life everyone else wants you to live instead of creating your own amazing life.

Chapter 1

The Perpetual Wheel

Come unto me, all you who are tired to the bone, and I will give you rest. –Jesus

I remember a time back when we were kids that my little sister and I got a great idea. We decided that we wanted pets of our own. We had recently been to a neighbor's house and had discovered something called a "Teddy Bear Hamster". We conspired how to convince the folks to take us to the pet store, and consequently get them to fall in love with our new prospective pets. We would suggest a Family Night Out—first dinner, and then a trip to the Pet Store (just to "look.") It was a foolproof plan!

Our parents fell for it, and out to dinner we went. After we finished dinner, we headed to the pet store around the corner. "Now remember, girls, we are just looking. We aren't going to come home with a new puppy like last time, okay?" Dad reminded. "Oh, we know, Dad!" I said, as my sister nodded enthusiastically in agreement.

When we got to the pet store, we walked in as calmly and coolly as possible. We casually looked around, trying not to be too eager about our real goal. We eventually made our way to the cages that held what we hoped would be our future pets. I think Mom and Dad were surprised at how cute they were, and we must have been extremely adorable that day, as well as convincing. We gave them that age-old pitch, "We need to learn how to be responsible, and we promise to feed them, and love them, and hold them, and clean up after them....blah, blah, blah." Mom looked at Dad. Dad looked at Mom. We looked at each other, crossing our fingers behind our backs. "Pleeez let us each get one Mom, pleeeeeez," I begged. I don't know if we caught them in a weak moment, or if they were just totally cool parents (which they are), but they fell for it. About a half hour later we were on our way home with creatures, cages, food, and all kinds of paraphernalia.

My little fluff ball was adorable. I named her Peaches. We were so happy to have our very own pet that we could keep in our rooms. We began putting together our hamsters' cages. Part of the necessary equipment that we brought home from the pet store was a small metal "wheel" that was attached to a base. The purpose of this wheel was to make sure the hamster got enough exercise. It was explained to us that although they liked being in a small space for safety, they had a definite need for activity.

We felt so grown up! We were officially pet owners. We could not have been more excited. That is, until we discovered, purely by accident, that hamsters are nocturnal. They are up all night and sleep all day. Now, that may not seem like a big problem. After all, how much of a disturbance could a creature of that size cause anyway. Well, we would soon find out.

That first night, still basking in the newness of my tiny friend, I said good night, turned out the light and crawled into my own soft bed. I drifted into that land between waking and sleeping. I was soon jarred awake by a persistent squeaking sound. I thought, "What in the world is that awful sound? Is Peaches dying?"

I flew out of bed to see what was wrong with my new pet! I flipped on the light to discover that Peaches had discovered her exercise wheel, and she was making the most of it. I watched in fascination as she frantically ran, causing the wheel to spin around and around, faster and faster. I wondered, "How much fun can that be? She's running in place as fast as she can! How long she can keep that up? Maybe she'll get tired."

At this point, I still didn't realize what "nocturnal" meant. It became clear that after a couple of hours of listening to that squeaking wheel go around and round that she could continue this for a very long time.

Luckily, like any other constant noise, you eventually get accustomed to it, just like the creaks of an old house, the furnace going on and off, or the sound of the nearby trains. After a few nights, it became "normal". I was able to sleep through it, but I never did quite comprehend why my little friend was content to work so hard, for so long, to get nowhere.

Fast forward 5 years. I was in 15 and in high school, and I was already on a wheel of my own. I was quite sensitive, extremely caring, and very much a people-pleaser. Doing the right thing was important. Looking the right way was important. Being a good student was important. Making everyone happy was important. Whether it was other people's expectations, or just my own of myself, it felt like a lot of pressure.

Fast forward 5 more years. I was a new bride, expecting my life of bliss with my Prince Charming. Once again, I stepped onto that wheel. Not only did I want to be the perfect wife, but I had just married a religion student who would soon be pastoring a church of his own; that made me a soon-to-be pastor's wife. Wow, even more pressure. Bigger expectations from my husband, myself, and more people.

Fast forward 4 more years. Now I was a mom. It's all I ever wanted, but now I had more responsibility, more tasks, and another person depending on me. I was overwhelmed. A husband, a household, a baby, church people, relationships, expectations, roles… I just didn't know how I would ever get it all done and keep everyone happy.

Dress up, show up, do what you're supposed to do. It was important to me to make sure that all my relationships were running smoothly, and I was willing to do pretty much whatever it took to make sure that happened. I tried harder. I did more. Yet, it never seemed like it was enough.

One day I stopped and looked at myself in the mirror. I was haggard. I was exhausted. I was running in circles, frantically, and I wasn't sure if I was getting anywhere. It was like deja vu. I had a memory of my childhood pet, Peaches, frantically running. I finally knew what it felt like to be on the Perpetual Wheel.

Swallowed Up

A Day in My Chaotic Life

So, what does a day look like on a Perpetual Wheel? Well, here's what mine looked like. As soon as I opened my eyes, I would begin to feel:

Depression like a dark cloud engulfing me.
Fatigue so heavy it was as if I had lead in my shoes.
Anxiety so permeating that I felt I would crawl out of my skin.
Frustration overwhelming me, like a thick fog you can't see through.
Apprehension suffocating me, as if someone's fingers were around my neck.
Dread so dark I longed to close my eyes, pull the blanket over my head, and shut out the world.

The hardest part for me to understand was there was nothing awful going on in my life except that I was so overwhelmed with how to keep everyone happy that I felt depressed and exhausted. I was convinced whatever we were experiencing, albeit stressful, was just life. I remember looking in the mirror while I put on my makeup in the mornings. I was going through the motions, trying to get myself psyched up for the day. I would look into my own eyes, disgusted with myself that I didn't have more energy, or a better attitude about things. I had conversations in my head while I looked at my stooped shoulders and bloodshot eyes; "Angie, what is your problem? You have people around you who love you. You have a beautiful child. You have a place to live and food to eat. You have God in your life. Pull it together. Your life is pretty darn good."

As I got in the car to run errands, I would once again catch a glimpse of my tired self and start in again, "You have a husband who loves you, he's not perfect, but he works hard. He loves your son. You could be a lot worse off! You have got to snap out of this funk. Stop being so depressed and ungrateful."

I found myself almost being irritated when I would see someone at the store or on the street smiling or laughing. "How come I don't feel like that?" I would think to myself. "You're just choosing to be miserable, and you're the only one who can change that," I thought, chastising myself. "You should be glad that you have a church full of people who care and that your husband gets to do what he loves. Why are you so selfish? When you got married, you knew this was going to be your life. You agreed to support him. Get over yourself."

Fast forward another year. We had another child, our baby girl. Life moved on. I continued to fulfill my roles and try to keep up and keep everyone happy.

Two and a half years after our second child was born, we were called from our first senior pastorate in Kansas City to Alaska to pastor another church. It seemed we were living the life we had planned and always wanted. But I was still exhausted and unfulfilled. I was still having those harsh conversations with myself that I hoped would motivate me out of that dark place, but it wasn't working at all. "Don't be a victim, Angie," I said to myself. "Lord knows how much those kind of people get on your nerves." The self-talk would continue, "You always tell your kids that their attitude is their choice, so it's time to take your own advice and fix yours. Maybe you're just not being a very good Christian, otherwise, you wouldn't be so miserable." I tried so hard to snap myself out of this funk, and it just wasn't working. The fact that I didn't have anything concrete to attribute my feelings to made it that much harder for me to understand and justify it. Every day I tried to figure out what I was doing wrong. I wanted so desperately to have an answer for this dark state I was in. Yet every day I came to the same conclusion, obviously, I was not measuring up in some way.

I spent every day trying to make sure I did enough so I felt valuable. I had chosen to support my husband in getting his schooling, following his dream, and building his career. This meant being the mostly stay-at-home parent, and there isn't a whole lot of value placed on that task most of the time. At times, it was easy to feel that perhaps my life just wasn't as significant and valuable as his because I was not contributing financially or making a huge impact on the world. However, I had chosen this, and I was determined to make the best of it.

At that time in my life, it was my number one priority to make sure everyone was happy; with me, with my husband, with my kids, with their lives... You can see why every day felt so overwhelming. No wonder I had anxiety about "getting it all done" and "making it all work" and "making sure everything looks perfect". Who wouldn't be exhausted, anxious, frustrated, depressed, and dreading waking up each day?

The most exhausting part was that it never felt like I could do enough to live up to this crazy standard I had set for myself. Who could? And who was asking how I was doing? What I needed? What I wanted in life? Well, as I said before, those things were irrelevant. "Who really cares, Angie," my critical self would pipe up, "It's not about you, remember. Just keep giving and serving, and loving, and maybe one day it will be enough." And so continued my life on the Perpetual Wheel.

The End of My Chaotic Day

You would think that the end of the day would be a welcome relief and at least a temporary reprieve from all of the expectations and roles, but it really wasn't much better than the way I woke up. In fact, it was a little worse because there was nothing left at all in my already lacking emotional tank. It makes sense that if you feel exhausted at the start of the day, it's only going to be magnified upon retiring, and I was. And yet, as exhausted as I was, the voice of my inner critic took this prime opportunity when it was quiet to chime in and cause me to question what I had even accomplished that day. More doubt, more guilt, more depression, anxiety, sleeplessness, and sadness. It reminded me of that wheel: running, striving, trying, expending, and not knowing if I had gotten anywhere or if I had created anything valuable. I had this deep, unsettled feeling, wondering if there was more, if there was a better way. This only caused more guilt over not being grateful for what I had.

As I drifted off into a fitful sleep, I dreaded the thought of another chaotic day that felt pointless. It seemed like there were just no answers. This left me utterly empty and quite hopeless that it would ever be better. The only conclusion I could come to was that it must be about me not doing enough or being enough. The only thing I knew to do was to try harder. But how. How would I do that? I had no idea.

What About You?

Does any of this sound familiar? Do you ever feel like you are on that wheel, going around and round and getting nowhere? Do you wish you could change it, but you have no idea how? Well my friend, there is hope, and there are answers. Life is hard. People are imperfect. Things don't go the way we think they should sometimes; most of the time. However, there is more to life than striving. There is more to you than fulfilling roles and giving until you break. There is a lot in this life that you can't control, but you are not powerless. You can love yourself and others at the same time. You can create a good life and relationships that are reciprocal. It will take work. It will take changes. It will take time. But it is possible. That's what this book is about. Setting limits. Taking your life back. Empowering others to take their lives back. Finding ways that actually work. Keep reading. You can do this.

Chapter 2

This Isn't Working!

We cannot solve our problems with the same thinking we used when we created them. -Albert Einstein

I'm so grateful that so many things in my life have changed. I'm so glad that I don't try to live my life the way I used to on that perpetual wheel. It has been a long journey, and I continue to learn all the time. Things are so much better now, because I've been willing to take an honest look at my life and not continue behaviors and patterns that don't work. Let's look at some of the things I finally realized were not serving me back in the beginning days of awareness.

Trying Harder.

Do you feel like no matter how much you do, it's just never quite enough? Not enough for you. Not enough for those around you. Not enough for God. What a frustrating place to be! Why do you assume that if something isn't working that the best solution is to try harder? To work more. To give more. To run farther. Strive, strive, strive. It's so exhausting.

It makes sense why you would think that trying harder is a solution. You've heard phrases like:

"The early bird gets the worm."
"Nothing worth having comes easy."
"There's nothing worse than a quitter."
"No pain, no gain."

You can probably add some of your own to this list. Here are some examples of "trying harder":

-Caring more about someone than they care about themselves. (Projecting)

-Suffering consequences for someone else's behavior because you feel some twisted sense of responsibility to make up for what they aren't doing that is their responsibility. (Buffering)

-Trying to rescue and enable and save other people from the consequences of their choices, and neglecting your own self. (Overly responsible)

-Staying in relationships that would not even exist if it wasn't for you holding them together. (Indispensable)

-Sacrificing and giving and doing even when it isn't appreciated or reciprocated. (Needing to be needed)

-Perpetuating the irresponsibility of other people who are okay with letting you pick up the slack for them. (Getting in the way)

This is the kind of trying harder that doesn't help anyone, not them, and especially not you. You can do it for a while, but you will wear down, burn out, and it will not be effective.

Why is it that you think that simply trying harder will fix whatever is wrong in your life and in the lives of others? Do you think it's like that old saying, "If a little is good, more must be better?" The problem is, when we are caught up in co-dependent or pleasing behavior, even a little bit is not good.

About 15 years into my marriage, I began to realize that what I thought were health issues, crazy accidents, and intermittent periods on narcotics and stimulants had become an addictive cycle for my husband.

He had been so functional and a master at hiding his substance abuse that I didn't even realize there was a problem.

When it finally got to the point he couldn't cover it up completely, it started to affect him and our family. First in small ways, then in greater ones.

Swallowed Up

When things really started to spiral out of control, I spent a lot of time, energy, and thought on figuring out how to make our lives function in spite of him. I felt that this was my responsibility as the wife and mother. I was the one bearing the torch of hope and normalcy for the family. Being hopeful and optimistic about things is a great trait, and it's needed in a family. The problem is, you can carry even a good thing too far.

At one point, about a year and a half before we split up, things had really come to a head with the addiction. The implications of my husband's substance abuse were beginning to become unmanageable for him, and I met with a friend of my sister who was a recovering addict of 25 years. I admit, even after all the years of living with it, I was still extremely naïve about what it meant to deal with someone with an addictive personality. As I met with this man, he began to ask me questions to try to get an idea of where things were at and how he could help, even if to just bring a bit more clarity and understanding.

I'm sure he could tell by the look on my face as he talked that I really had no idea exactly what we were dealing with and at what level. I appreciated that in spite of my dropped jaw and the tears running down my face that he did not try to sugarcoat anything for me. He was compassionate. He could see my pain, but he knew that I needed understanding, and he continued to be truthful in a kind way. I remember one thing he said to me that practically took my breath away. He asked me "Well, have you ever just gotten out of the way and let him fall?" I was speechless. He repeated the question. After a long pause I finally answered, "Well, of course not, that wouldn't be right. I'm his wife. I can't do that". He proceeded to explain to me that as long as I continued to buffer for my husband, he would never feel the pain that was necessary for him to do anything different. It made sense, but I couldn't fathom how I would ever be okay with that.

It took me several days of processing, but I began to realize, and I realize even more now what I had been doing. I was trying harder to make everything work and it wasn't working.

I was projecting. I cared about my husband and our family so much and I wanted desperately for him to do what he needed to do so that we would all be okay.

I was buffering. Due to the fact that I am such a highly empathetic person, seeing someone else in pain actually causes me emotional or physical pain. Deep down inside I think I knew that he should suffer the consequences of his behavior, but I just didn't want him to. I also understood that his choices directly affected the family, so I knew he would not be the only one suffering. So I protected him as much as I could. Hardly anyone knew what was going on, especially the kids. I thought it was my job to protect all of them, and was I wrong?

I was overly responsible. What choice did I have? I was the only one making rational decisions most of the time. At this point, the addiction had taken over and he wasn't even the person I knew; but I was still hopeful he would come around and come back to us.

I was indispensable. Someone had to hold things together and try to provide some sense of stability, and he just didn't have the capacity to do that at this point. He spent most of his days influenced by the prescription drugs, or feeling so much shame that he didn't want to be alive. It was hardly a relationship. At that point, I couldn't leave. I knew if I did, he would never be okay, the kids would be from a "broken home", I couldn't support us financially, and above all else, I had said "Til death do us part", and I had meant it. The crazy part was I had already grieved the loss of him long before now. It seemed as if the person I had married and spent so many years with didn't exist anymore.

I needed to be needed. As I said before, I became very good at playing roles and making sure that everyone around me was okay and as happy as possible. I found my value in pouring into others' lives, because I was convinced that giving was always the answer to every problem.

I was getting in the way. There was no way that his behavior was going to change. Why should it? It was working for him, even though it wasn't working for me. Yet, I continued to step between him and any discomfort and hoped that somehow he would just wake up one day and decide to make different choices.

Why Trying Harder Doesn't Work

It's draining. It takes a lot of energy to push yourself harder and harder all the time.

It's frustrating. You feel like you continue to do more and more, and it doesn't produce the results you want.

It's distracting. Our culture is very focused on DOING. You value people who get things done. You lift up the people with lots of energy who seem to be going somewhere with their lives. But doing also is a way of not evaluating what's happening. It may make you feel productive, but the truth is you may be avoiding the real issue and the reality of the situation.

It's boring. There's just nothing very inspiring and motivating about doing the same thing for a long time and not seeing progress. Remember the wheel?

It's futile. Who cares if you're going fast if you are going nowhere. You won't do well if you don't see progress.

It's not meant to be. Maybe it's not your path, maybe you are wasting your energy on the wrong thing. Maybe it's keeping you from the right thing.

Sometimes you do get what you want and to where you want by trying harder, but not always. Think about how ridiculous it would be to tell someone who had their car stuck in the mud that if they just try harder they will eventually get out.

If you have ever been in this predicament, what is your first inclination? To step on the gas, right? Just power your way out. But realistically, what happens when you do that? Sometimes just the opposite happens and the wheels end up sinking farther into the slime. You actually end up digging a deeper trench than was there in the first place.

Once you've spent a while trying to force your way out of the mud, you probably figure out that it's not working. It doesn't matter how much someone encourages you to try harder, it's just not happening. So what's the answer? First of all, you need to stop. Your smarts and your power and your reliable car are not going to cut it this time. You need to assess the situation. If you're stuck in the mud, the answer is going to be to get some help to get out. You probably need something bigger than your car to do that. If you can't get someone to help, you will at least have to figure out how to get some traction. You are going to have to try differently. Trying harder is not going to change others or even circumstances sometimes, especially when it comes to relationship which takes two people giving and trying.

What's The Alternative?

If what you are doing isn't working, and trying harder is definitely not working, you will have to do something different if you want a different result. Here's a few more practical suggestions that just may help:

Stop. You need to interrupt this ineffective pattern. The only way to do that is to quit doing what you're doing and figure out what's wrong

Evaluate. Figure out what path led to the swamp. How did you get here? What happened? If you don't figure this out, you will probably end up doing the same thing or something else that doesn't work.

Realize that you cannot make up for someone else's irresponsibility. You trying harder is not going to change others or even circumstances if others are involved.

Understand you cannot make a relationship work by yourself. A relationship takes two people giving and trying.

Minimizing

Minimizing is "not recognizing or acknowledging something for what it truly is." It is a form of denial, and I have used it a lot during my life. Possibly many of you have as well. Why do you do this? Most psychologists and therapists agree that the biggest reason is to decrease the intensity of a situation. You use it as a numbing technique so that you can convince yourself and others that things aren't as bad as they seem. It is actually a form of what is referred to in the field of psychology as cognitive distortion--using inaccurate thoughts to convince yourself that something isn't really true. While it may temporarily relieve your anxiety, it definitely is not based in reality, and eventually that becomes a problem.

Here are a few ways that you may tend to minimize things when you don't want to face reality:

-Justifying - You cover over poor behavior (yours or someone else's) by making excuses or giving explanations. Saying things like "everyone has issues" and convincing yourself that whatever the behavior is must be "normal."

-Over-hoping- (I don't know if it's officially a word, but it is for our purposes!) - You know that if you just wait a little longer, be a little more positive, and keep on hoping that things will just get better on their own....magically.

-Comparing - You compare yourself to others or your experiences to others experiences to show yourself that things aren't really that bad. After all, you can always find someone worse off than you are, right?

-Disregarding - You downplay or don't validate your feelings or the feelings of others. You tell yourself or others that you/they shouldn't feel that way.

-Masking – You pretend like everything is fine, even good when you know it isn't. It's the ultimate form of faking it, and it's exhausting.

When I was in the process of trying to "save" my 23+ year marriage, I spent several weeks seeing a marriage counselor. My whole goal was to figure out what I needed to do to make things work, and I planned on getting some tools through counseling to do exactly that.

At the first session, the Counselor asked me questions so I could give him a picture of our situation. I was distraught on the inside because we were currently separated (though not officially). But I had become masterful at this skill of minimizing, and it showed up in my session, even though I really had nothing to lose by telling my counselor exactly how things were. I proceeded to explain in a nutshell about the past 15 years of addiction that had led us to this point. I did what I normally do, even when I'm dying inside. I used humor, tried to highlight the good as much as I shared the bad, and because I don't like to be a "downer". I turned on the bubbles and positivity. I didn't see this as fake at all, because it had become such a part of who I was. It was my coping strategy, and I had become very proficient at it.

I explained where things were at in our relationship. I told him what we had been through in the past couple of years with my husband's addiction that had spiraled out of control. I told him how it had affected our family, me, and especially him. I had snapped, and I knew something had to change. I had left and gone to a friend's house because he had stayed out all night and then lied to me about it.

After I got done giving him the Reader's Digest version of my crazy life, I said, "Well, I guess that's about it." He sat quietly for a moment. It seemed like forever to me. He thoughtfully and empathetically asked me, "So, how does all of that make you feel?" I thought for a moment, and with little to no emotion I responded, "Well, it really hurts." Silence....then he spoke again, "Really? That's so interesting, because you just said that with a smile." It hit me like a ton of bricks. I had no idea that I was smiling. I was sobbing on the inside, but you would never be able to tell that by just looking at me. When he said that, I melted into tears, and then sobs.

I'm pretty sure he didn't actually say this, but after all of the people I've worked with and coaching I've done, I know he thought the same thing that I think when someone finally lets down the mask and gets real, "Now I've got something to work with." I wasn't intentionally trying to hide or lie or be in denial. I obviously wanted help or I wouldn't have sought out counseling. I was just doing what I had done for so many years, I was minimizing, justifying, hoping, and just trying to hold my fragile world together.

I had figured out a way to numb out the reality of my life so that I could just keep moving forward, and it had worked for a long time. I used all of the tactics mentioned above to buffer myself and others from the pain that I was so afraid to face. Anyone who has lived with someone addicted to any kind of substance or behavior understands what I mean.

-I excused his poor behavior and blamed it on his troubled childhood. (Justifying).

-I took on the role of holding out hope for his recovery, even though he was not willing to admit or deal with his issues. (Over-hoping). (The same therapist told me I had more "pathological hope" than anyone he had ever met, and no, that is not a good thing!)

-I compared myself and our lives to others and came to the conclusion that it could be a lot worse and I should be grateful. (Comparing).

-I shamed myself for having any negative emotions at all. After all, what was the value in having a pity party about my situation? (Disregarding).

-I always portrayed to everyone around me, including our children, that everything was great. We had the image of a very happy and functional family because I made sure we appeared that way. (Masking).

No, I wasn't able to "save" our marriage. In the months following our divorce, I learned a lot of people were not shocked by it. Some were. But the people that had been observing us more closely over the past 10 years saw through the façade I tried to keep in place. They didn't know exactly what was going on, but they knew that something wasn't right.

Why Minimizing Doesn't Work.

It prolongs the inevitable.

It interrupts the learning process (choices=consequences).

It keeps you in the dark (you can't fix what you don't acknowledge).

It perpetuates poor behavior.

It allows you to lie to yourself.

It keeps you stuck.

It keeps you in pain.

It causes you not to trust yourself.

What's The Alternative?

Be willing to look at what you are fearful about.

Ask yourself, "What could NOT taking action cost me?" as opposed to asking what it will cost you to face it.

Allow yourself to feel your feelings and experience your emotions.

Try to figure out what beliefs you have that are irrational.

Do some journaling. This is a safe way to face your fears and relieve your anxiety. It may also help you to sort it all out and come up with solutions to the problem.

Talk to someone you trust; a friend, or a coach or a therapist who can help you be objective about the situation.

Find a support group that deals with your specific situation. You may find it helpful to hear other people's stories and get input on what they are doing to cope.

Minimizing is a form of denial, and believe it or not it does serve a purpose. Denial is a built in protective system that makes it possible for you to realize and deal with loss and trauma while not allowing it to totally take you out. If you experienced the full impact of the traumatic experience or the great loss all at once, you would not be able to handle it, physically or emotionally. Denial is a buffer, if you will, to help you through the grief process, and it does a good job of protecting.

The problem with denial as with any other behavior that keeps you from dealing with reality is that you can't stay there; not if you want to be emotionally healthy. There is a time to deny and a time to acknowledge. There is a time to distract yourself and a time to face the truth. There is a time to get your mind off of the negative and a time to be introspective. There is a time to feel and a time to think.

Facing the truth about someone or a situation is not easy. But it is necessary in order to move ahead with a healthy perspective. It's all about balance, and making sure you are moving through whatever it is, and not getting stuck in it.

Martyr Syndrome

A person with a martyr syndrome puts everyone else's needs above his or her own so that he or she can suffer for the sake of others and thus give his or her life meaning. Speaking from personal experience, I believe it is possible to do this without even intending to. Let me explain.

I remember coming to a point in my life that I felt powerless in every way. I realize now that even though there are a lot of things I didn't' have power over, there were areas I did have some. I just didn't realize it. Until I understood this, however, I honestly felt like I was at the mercy of the people and circumstances in my life.

Now that I have been working on myself, doing personal development work, going to therapy, facilitating classes on setting boundaries and life-coaching, I understand that I was "giving my power away". I now know that I was "teaching people how to treat me". I get that I am "responsible for my own happiness", and I can choose who I want to be in my life, but I really did not understand that back then. I just figured that my relationships and my circumstances were part of my destiny, and I needed to have a good attitude and make the best of it. How devastating it was for me when I realized I just couldn't do it that way anymore.

Why the Martyr Complex Doesn't Work

You give our power away.

You do things for the wrong reasons (You say yes when you want to say no, which is not honest).

You do things out of fear instead of out of love.

You do things because you are trying to make up for something (low self-esteem).

You do more than you should or want to because it seems "spiritual".

You think you are a victim, that you have no choices, that this is just "the way it is", your "lot in life." This makes it easier to blame others than to take responsibility for your own life.

You try to do more in order to earn the love you desire from others and God.

You create drama and try to get your needs met by manipulation.

Have you ever known anyone who suffered with a martyr complex? It can be annoying. It also can be very sad. The worst part is that a lot of times the person who takes it on may not even realize what they're doing. A lot of times people equate martyrdom with spirituality, and it's understandable. After all, even the Bible tells us to "take up our cross." So, if it seems like such a noble and admirable trait, why doesn't it work?

Mother Teresa is considered one of the most amazing human beings to have ever lived. She is the ultimate example of someone who literally gave up their own wants, needs, pleasures, and happiness in order to live a life of servitude. We can definitely learn from her successes and also from her struggles.

At first she was a teacher, which in itself is a selfless calling. I don't know that there is a more underappreciated, underpaid position in this world, and yet the impact a teacher can have is probably the most powerful next to a parent. She taught until she received a "second call" as she referred to it. She felt absolutely called by God to leave her life and her teaching at the school to live and serve in the slums which housed the sickest and most impoverished people.

She received only six months of very basic medical training before going to the slums of Calcutta, where she had only one aspiration; to serve the unwanted, the unloved, the abandoned, the sick and the very, very poor.

There was a dark side to all of this, which most did not even realize or begin to understand until after her death in 1997: She suffered from deep depression and disconnection for the very God she served.

In one despairing letter to a confidant, Mother Teresa wrote, *"Where is my Faith--even deep down right in there is nothing, but emptiness & darkness--My God--how painful is this unknown pain--I have no Faith--I dare not utter the words & thoughts that crowd in my heart--& make me suffer untold agony."* (from the book "Come Be My Light").

I chose Mother Teresa as an example, because it really begs the question: Is it possible to fulfill your call, be obedient to God, live a life of humble service, and yet not lose yourself entirely?

It just seems like there should be a way to love others and also love yourself. I find it hard to believe God would not want us to experience the very thing that is He is trying to accomplish through us. After all, He made us, and He knows that we all have needs, and it just makes sense that if He asks us to meet the needs of others, He wants our needs to be met as well.

Mother Teresa reached more people than you will ever be able to count or realize, and yet at what cost? Could this have been done without sacrificing her very health and soul? I would like to think instead of an "either/or" situation that it could have been a "both/and", and I do believe it can be for you and me.

What did she do that didn't work so well? What caused her to feel the despair, abandonment, and the "not enough' feelings that are apparent in her candid writings that have now become public?

She probably felt powerless. She did give her power away when she pledged a life of service, poverty, and humility. Perhaps her belief in "the call" caused her to believe that this was her "lot in life" and her job was to be obedient and make the best of it.

I also can see how her vows were probably the primary motivation to live her life in this way. Therefore, she did many things out of obligation and fear of not doing enough rather than coming strictly from love.

It is also apparent from her writings that she did not feel worthy of anything, including the love and favor of God, which may indicate that she had a low self-esteem. She seemed to suffer from not feeling "enough" most of the time.

Was her expectation of herself, living up to what she thought that meant was, actually more than God ever expected or requires from one person? He wanted her to be served and cared for as well. Regardless, her firm belief was that she had to do what seemed to be practically impossible in order to fulfill her "spiritual" duties.

Did she feel that she had to earn the love of God by DOING? She didn't seem concerned about the approval or accolades of man. She wanted to be loved and approved by God more than anything.

An Aha Moment.

I had a wonderful friend and mentor, who is also brilliant psychologist say to me one time during a therapy session, "Angie, there's nothing you can do that will cause God to love you less, and there's nothing you can do that will cause God to love you more." Really? I didn't have to earn God's love and approval? Then I got to thinking, well that would be kind of ridiculous. If God is my Father and I am His child, He loves me, period. Just like I love my kids. Do I always approve or agree with what they're doing or the decisions their making? No. But what does that have to do with my love for them? Nothing! Their behavior may make me sad or disappointed or angry, but it doesn't change my love for them. And that's how God feels about me. How cool is that?

What's The Alternative?

Be sure you are speaking your truth along with being a great listener. This is the key to good communication. It's so important to be clear about what's important to you, what you are willing to do, and what needs you have that you want to be met.

Realize you don't have to say yes to everything. You do not always have to be "the one" to help. If you feel like your heart is telling you to help and it's coming from love, by all means, say yes. But also be very aware if you are tempted yes out of obligation or pressure. If you feel resentful at the thought of giving to a person or in a situation, that may be a pretty good indicator that you should say no and let someone else step up.

Stop expecting to be rewarded. If you are doing something in order to receive something in return, you may want to rethink your motivation. Remember that a gift is just that, a gift. There shouldn't be strings attached.

Sacrifice versus suffering. If your giving moves from sacrifice to suffering, you may be giving for the wrong reasons. If you are suffering as a result of helping someone else, you may be being codependent and enabling, and that is not good for anyone involved.

Stop making your primary goal to please and avoid conflict. It's okay if people are disappointed, hurt or even angry when you say no. It's impossible to make everyone happy all the time. Ask your heart what you should do instead of listening to all of the noise and opinions around you.

Self-care. Not only is it healthy, it is necessary if you want to continue to give and serve at your highest capacity. You wouldn't expect your car to run on an empty tank, so why do you think that you can? Every day, take some time to do something that feeds your soul, rests your body, or sparks your passion.

The intention of this particular section is to help you see that although martyrdom is A WAY, it is not the most effective way. If you feel like you're only option is to sacrifice your whole self for a cause or a person, then you have to decide that. However, I do believe there is a better way.

Would you agree that we should always be grateful and good stewards of everything we have been given? And do you agree that a person who is not grateful or a good steward does not deserve to be given better and more if they are not able to take care of what they have?

Your body, mind, and soul are the most precious gifts that you have been given. They are what give you the ability and the capacity to give whatever you have been placed in this world to give. We all have the responsibility to nurture, protect, care for, and use wisely all of ourselves so that we can create the value we are intended to create. If you don't self-care, you are limiting the possibilities of giving and serving to the extent that you were meant to.

Do you ever think you are doing yourself, others, and even God a favor by neglecting yourself--sacrificing at great lengths, denying your needs and even your wants--when in reality you are doing exactly the opposite?

Your body, mind, and soul is amazing and powerful, and they deserve to be honored and cherished so that they can serve you well in order that you might serve others well.

Stuffing

What does stuffing even mean? Suppressing, repressing, denying, ignoring, or invalidating our emotions. If you've ever done this before, you know what I'm talking about. It even works, for a while. It seems like a reasonable solution. I mean after all, you can't just go around spewing out your feelings all the time on the poor people around you. You think if you push those feelings down or put them aside, perhaps they will just magically dissipate and you won't ever have to pull them out into the open and deal with them. How convenient. Too bad that's not the way it works.

Unfortunately, emotions can only be stuffed down for so long. There's only so much "space" inside you to continue to compound your pain. I remember one of the first times I decided to try counseling, after my doctor suggested it would help me. I remember being a little afraid to share the analogy of how I was feeling with my counselor, for fear they would decide I needed to be "put somewhere safe where I could be observed." I finally decided that if I wasn't crazy already, I would definitely be there soon, so I decided I didn't have a lot to lose.

I remember saying to the counselor, "I just feel like I've pushed my feelings down for so long, that there's just no more room inside for me to stuff one more thing." I remember putting the back of my hand up to my chin and saying, "I mean it's literally like they are up to here, and I could just start throwing up at any moment." That's how visceral the feeling of being literally filled to the top with pain was in that moment for me. I felt physically ill. The counselor didn't pick up the phone to call the men with the white jackets. His eyes didn't get big, and his jaw didn't drop. He said, "Well, I think that's a pretty good description, and it's also pretty normal." I'm never sure how to feel when a therapist tells you that what you've said is "normal" considering the people he sees all day long, but I decided that it was good that I didn't totally shock him.

I've learned over the years that when you think you are ignoring or avoiding your emotions and that it is an effective way to deal with your pain that you are actually deluding yourself. There is really only one way to deal with your pain and your emotions, and that is to feel them and work through them. I know that's not what people want to hear, especially if they have been through things that have been ugly and traumatic. It seems like a way better idea to just move on and try to forget, but it just doesn't work that way.

I have found this especially true when it comes to the emotions of anger and grief. It's a strange phenomenon, but one that has been confirmed to me over and over. Here's what I've discovered; it doesn't matter whether something happened 20 minutes ago or 20 years ago, when it eventually comes up (which it will) it will be equally as painful as when it initially occurred. I don't know that I can even explain why this is, I just know that it is true. When it comes to these two powerful emotions, there is no other option than to face and deal with them, and the sooner the better.

The illustration I will use may leave you thinking "I could have gone my whole life without hearing that," but I think it makes a good point. Years ago, our family was invited to dinner at another family's house from our church. When we came into the house, we removed our shoes because it was quite rainy and muddy outside on that particular day. After the lovely dinner, we made our way into the living room to play some board games and visit. I walked across the floor to admire some family photos that were displayed on the mantle above the fireplace. As I did this in my stocking feet, my foot came down on something sharp and it hurt something fierce. I sat down on the floor, took off my sock and examined my foot carefully to see what the culprit of my pain was. I could see that something was in my foot, and I bravely pulled it out. It ended up being part of a toothpick that had worked its way into the carpet and had been there for who knows how long. As you can imagine, my foot was very sore for several days. In fact, it was still sore even after several weeks, but I didn't think much of it considering a toothpick is a pretty large and sharp thing for a foot to recover from. I don't know if I just kind of forgot about it and got used to it being sore, but one day I stepped down on it and felt excruciating, shooting pain. I knew that this wasn't right, and it had been way too long for it to still be the wound from that toothpick I had stepped on months earlier. Once again, I sat down, removed my sock and looked carefully at my foot. It had been a while since I had examined it, and I noticed that there was still a hole where I had pulled the toothpick out. The area all the way around this hole was quite red compared to the rest of my foot. I started to push around on it a little bit to try to assess what was going on, and as I did., the rest of that toothpick I had stepped on months before popped out. It had festered and festered until the slightest pressure caused it to be expelled from my poor foot. Needless to say, I was totally freaked out, but then I realized how much better my foot felt immediately!

Can I tell you how good it felt to get that out of my body? I had ignored and minimized and discounted the irritation I had been feeling, because I knew it would eventually just go away, but the problem was there was still a foreign object in there, and my foot was not going to stop hurting until it was removed. The same is true with your painful emotions. You may try to ignore, or put salve on, or cover over those wounds, but the culprit of your pain is still there. Until you get to the root of the problem, it will continue to fester and cause pain. Until you deal with it, it will not have the opportunity to heal. The good news is, once you recognize it, treat it, do surgery on it, or whatever is necessary, it doesn't have the power to cause you that kind of pain anymore.

Why Stuffing Doesn't Work

You get more anxious.

You are MORE preoccupied subconsciously when we try to stuff it down.

You spend a lot of emotional energy suppressing.

It manifests eventually; often in the form of physical illness.

Others can't help and don't know how to help if we hide your emotions.

You get resentful, because it festers inside you.

Is it true that I could still function even though I had something in my foot that was causing pain and keeping me from operating at full capacity? Sure. And I did. But think of the discomfort, annoyance, readjusting I could have avoided if I would have known what was going on and gotten rid of it? It's the same in your life. You may be able to trudge along and ignore and suppress and still get things done, but how much freer, more productive, joyful, open, focused can you be on the things that matters to you could you be if you figured out healthy ways to deal with feelings, emotions and things that affect you a lot more than you are willing to admit they do?

Also, if you do the hard work of looking at those things that you are so afraid of, and then you actually work through them and clear them out of your life, how much more room will you have for the good things that are waiting for the opportunity to come into your life? As long as you hold on to old patterns and behaviors and stories, there is no time or room or opportunity for you to experience new ones.

Don't you think it's time to let those old stories go and write a new chapter for your life? You can hold on to the past if you want, and you will as long as you keep stuffing, but I wouldn't recommend it. You deserve better.

What's The Alternative?

Don't judge your feelings. They are not right or wrong, they just are. Feelings are amoral. They show up without your permission.

Feel your feelings. I know, it's not comfortable, but it's okay. Just sit with your feelings and allow them to flow through you instead of getting stuck.

Try to identify what the emotion actually is. Everyone has emotions they are more comfortable with than others. A lot of men are more comfortable with anger than they are with sadness. A lot of women are more comfortable with being depressed than with being angry. Sometimes when you are hurt it comes out as hostility and defensiveness. Start to be aware of what you are actually feeling and be okay with it. Then respond appropriately.

Refrain from numbing out your pain with substances, food, shopping, gambling, sleeping, or whatever vice you use to escape your discomfort. This isn't a solution, and the issue will still be there later, along with the guilt or remorse of whatever you were using to mask the pain.

Find a safe place to process. Reach out to a trusted friend, a coach, a counselor, a mentor. Join a support group with people that are dealing with similar challenges. It is rare for people to be able to work through and figure out everything on their own. You're too close to it. You need some objectivity. You need validation. You need input. I know it makes you vulnerable, but as my sister says, "We get messed up with people, and we get well with people."

If we do the hard work of looking at those things that we are so afraid of, and then we actually work through them and clear them out of our lives, how much more room will we have for the good things that are waiting for the opportunity to come into our lives? As long as we hold on to old patterns, behaviors, and stories, there is no time or room or opportunity for us to experience new ones. Isn't it time to let those old stories go and write a new chapter for your life? You can hold on to the past if you want, and you will as long as you keep stuffing, but I wouldn't recommend it.

Controlling

A lot of times when you feel like things are chaotic and out of control, you attempt to control more. You try to control other people and your surroundings. It makes sense that if the opposite of chaos is control you would naturally think this is the solution. There's just one problem--control is an illusion. You may think that you can control the people around you and make them do what you want and what you think is right. Unfortunately, it will break down your relationships, and chances are that it won't last. You really cannot control the people around you, and a lot of times you can't even control your circumstances or even your environment. The only thing you actually have control over is yourself.

Control is "the power to influence or direct people's behavior or the course of events." **Before you decide to skip over this section because you don't believe you are a controlling person, I challenge you to read on.** You see, there are a myriad of ways to be controlling besides the aggressive, domineering, overt way. So don't let yourself off the hook quite yet, because it may surprise you to find out that even submissive, silent, passive types have their own way of trying to control people and situations.

Here are some of the different ways we attempt to control:

Intimidation

Manipulation

Silent treatment

Withholding love (conditional love)

Emotional distance

Giving up

Perfectionism

Self-harm

Micromanaging

Isolating someone

Not validating feelings

Not listening (disregarding)

Not valuing someone's opinion (dismissing)

Fear

Guilt

Shame

Reverse psychology.

I guess you could argue that it is possible to control other people. You can manipulate, guilt, bully, coerce other people into doing what you want, but they are only one choice away from doing their own thing, and then you are back at square one again. People really need to be internally motivated to make lasting change, or it just doesn't stick. External motivation is not inspiring, and it rarely causes people to make sustainable changes in their lives no matter how much they should. That's why the idea of influence is so much more appealing in my mind. You can't force others to do what you would do, but you can definitely model and encourage positive, healthy choices and behaviors.

There are some things you can do to try to control your environment, and maybe it works to some extent. We all know people with Obsessive-Compulsive Disorder that clean, organize, alphabetize, plan, compartmentalize. The list goes on... Perhaps that does provide some semblance of order, but all it takes is for one thing to be out of place and their world comes crashing down. It also doesn't really do anything for the emotional pain or lack of limits in their lives, so it ends up being a pretty superficial solution for much deeper issues.

Why Controlling Doesn't Work

It's an illusion. You can't actually make anyone do anything.

People get resistant. They want to make their own choices and come up with their own answers.

People get resentful. No one likes to be dictated to. They want to be enrolled and included in the process of decision-making.

People get angry. It is frustrating to have someone bully you and try to force their beliefs and ideas on you.

It fractures relationships. A healthy relationship consists of both parties contributing, making decisions, having a voice, being respected, and being valued.

People get rebellious. It's human nature for us to want to push against strict codes and mandates, especially if we don't understand them or have a buy-in to them.

What's The Alternative?

Stop catastrophizing (which is a form cognitive distortion that means making things much bigger or worse than they are). Chances are the world will not come to an end if you can't control everyone and everything.

Stop being so suspicious. Give the benefit of the doubt. Everything is not about you. Everyone is not trying to sabotage your life and your success.

Pick your battles. Let go of what doesn't matter. You can be right every time if you want to, but realize you will probably be alone as well.

Let go of your expectations. You don't need to know or control the outcome of everything. It doesn't always have to go your way. Get over yourself! Learn to accept.

Relax. Switch roles; Let someone else take the reins and see how that feels. Who knows, you may enjoy not having to make it all work out!

Work on you and worry less about working on others. Your responsibility is YOU. Let others be responsible for themselves.

Practice respect. You have the right to make your own decisions about your life and what you are responsible for. Don't forget that others have that same right as well. Be respectful and accepting of others' choices even if you don't agree. It's none of your business.

Listen. Really listen. Not the type of listening where you wait for the person to finish so you can sell them on why your way is a better way. Listen with your heart and really hear what they are saying. You do not have all the answers, and you definitely don't know what's best for someone else.

Be teachable. You don't have to know everything, or always be the expert. Try to see things from other perspectives. Practice being open instead of being convinced that your way is the only/best way.

Give others the chance to shine and contribute. We are all different and have gifts to give to the world. Make sure you're not getting in the way of someone else having the opportunity to give their gifts.

Appreciate diversity. How boring would it be if everyone were the same? Our differences are what make life interesting and beautiful. After all, would you really want everyone to be just like you?

Stop trying to change people. No one wants to feel like they are "not enough" or that there is something wrong with them.

Control is a great thing when you need to hold yourself in check. Self-control can be very appropriate and valuable. You need to manage all your behavior, emotions, feelings, and responsibilities. Where you get into trouble is when you resort to other-control. Remember, it's not effective. It's not motivating. It may get you what you want temporarily, but it probably won't last. It will cost you intimacy in your relationships. It will stunt the growth of those around you who need to take responsibility for what's theirs and find their own way. Work on you. Love people. Influence people. Honor people. Breathe. Surrender. Live.

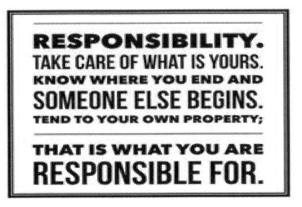

So Now What?

I imagine you may be feeling a little disheartened, even a little bit bogged down by all this talk about what's not working. I know it's not easy when we realize that we could have done things a lot better or at least a lot different. Don't give up! We have to identify what's not working so that we can start to implement different patterns. If anything, I hope you can see that there are legitimate reasons why you feel the way you do. Frustrated. Exhausted. Discouraged. Fed up. Directionless. Disrespected. Unappreciated.

If you will continue to be open and honest and willing to understand your patterns, to identify what's working and what isn't, and if you will commit to walking in the light that is shed by the truth about you and your relationships, you will begin to be hopeful. It's not an easy journey, but it will change your life if you are willing and you choose to stick it out. Don't quit! The best is yet to come! Now, let's figure out how to get off the wheel and find the path!

Swallowed Up

Chapter 3

Trading in the Wheel for a Path

When you lose something in your life, stop thinking it's a loss for you... it is a gift you have been given so you can get on the right path to where you are meant to go, not to where you think you should have gone.
-Suze Orman

Unless you are really paying attention to the way you are going about your life, you might not even understand the difference between being on a wheel and being on a path. I believe the reason for this is that there are similarities between the two.

Comparisons

Movement – It's true that whether you are on a perpetual wheel, or on a path, there is definitely movement.

Doing – Hey, it's not like my hamster, Peaches, was lying around eating bon bons and drinking fruity drinks, and neither are you! You have been doing a lot. It takes time, energy, and commitment. Those are all good things, right? And besides, it seems like something is happening as long as you are doing something.

Activity – This goes along with the doing part. We live in a culture that says:

"Find something to do."
"Keep your hands busy."
"There are always things to be done."

It's true that idleness isn't good for a person on a regular basis; physically, emotionally, spiritually. The problem is when we "mistake activity for accomplishment," as I have heard my father say so many times over the years. In other words, just because you are busy doesn't necessarily mean you are creating value.

Using Energy – There's no doubt that Peaches used vast amounts of energy on that wheel every day. I have no doubt that you are using a lot, too, in order to keep up with everything on your plate. It takes a lot of energy to sustain a pace like that. The question is: Are you using the limited energy you have (and everyone's amount and capacity is different depending on health, work, stage of life, and other factors) on things that will actually make a difference for you and for others?

Years ago, when I was married to my pastor husband, we moved to Washington State to pastor a congregation. The church provided a beautiful parsonage for us to live in right next door to the church. On the other side of the parsonage were some wonderful people who were also members of the church. The whole neighborhood was beautiful with well-kept older homes and mature trees.

In our yard, we had a huge tree that provided shade for almost the entire front lawn. It was a gorgeous tree. I loved it. Until fall. This tree had a bazillion (yes, a bazillion) small leaves that dropped for what seemed like months once autumn came. I have to admit that when I realized how futile it was to rake the leaves until they had all come down, I decided I would just live with leaves for a while.

There was just one problem. My neighbor, now retired, took great pride in having an absolutely immaculate lawn--one that included no fallen leaves. He diligently raked leaves every day, so I could not let mine pile up like I had intended because....well, you know. I was worried about what the other neighbors might think. It's kind of like when your neighbor mows the grass, and then your grass looks long all of a sudden. Yeah, like that.

I resigned myself to take a little time to rake every day to keep up with my dear neighbor. He was always pleased to see me, and we would chat, and sometimes he would even help. I soon realized after a few days that his trees had lost all of their leaves, and mine was far from it. It felt like each time I would get the leaves raked and bagged, I would come out a half hour later, and it would look like I had done nothing. The other thing that was so frustrating was that some days when I wasn't able to rake 5-6 times a day (I didn't really do this), a breeze would kick up and blow my leaves onto my neighbor's leaf-free lawn. He had a lot of time to look at his lawn, and I knew, as kind as he was that he would be happier if this did not happen. There were even times that he was so committed to keeping his lawn immaculate and leaf-free, and I was busy with kids or other things, I would come home to find that he had actually been over raking up MY leaves.

It was a lot of pressure trying to keep up on those tiny leaves! I remember one day in desperation going out and trying to figure out if there was a way to speed the process and shake all of the remaining leaves off the tree so I could be done with it! It seemed that no matter how committed I was, how many times I raked, and even how many times my neighbor helped, there were just always more of those darn leaves!

Does your life every feel that way? Do you ever feel like you are doing the same thing: persistently, diligently, faithfully, and tenaciously, and yet it just feels like you are still getting buried? It's frustrating, isn't it?

Maybe you have the same challenge that I did--as much as I wanted my neighbor to have a nice lawn and be happy, I just couldn't seem to keep up with the leaves! And at the end of the day, I couldn't help but think, "They're just leaves after all, it's not like it's going to hurt anybody!" I tend to be one of those people that wants to "make a difference" and "see people's lives change." I admit that I couldn't see how raking leaves for weeks on end would accomplish that! Sounds a lot like the perpetual wheel, doesn't it?

Contrasts

We talked above about how it is possible for the wheel and the path to seem similar. However, there are so many ways that they are extremely different, so let's talk about those.

Wheel	**Path**
Going nowhere (fast)	Going somewhere (paced)
Frantic	Grounded
Obscure (no direction)	Intentional (with direction)
Same scenery	New and changing perspective
Sprint	Marathon
Hoping for a result	Growing on the journey
Committed	Congruent (in alignment)
Restrictive	Progressive
Exhaustion	Fulfillment/Contentment

In contrast to the leaf story, I think about one of my favorite stories that you may be familiar with.

The Starfish Story (original story written by Loren Eisley)
One day a man was walking along the beach when he noticed a young boy picking something up and gently throwing it into the ocean. Approaching the boy, he asked, "What are you doing?" The boy replied, "I'm throwing these starfish back into the ocean. The surf is up and the tide is going out. If I don't throw them back, they will die."

"Son," the man said, "Do you realize that there are miles and miles of beach and hundreds of starfish? Do you really think that will make a difference?" After listening respectfully, the boy bent down, picked up another starfish, and threw it gently into the surf. Then, looking up at the man and smiling, he said "Well, it made a difference for that one!"

So what's the point of these two illustrations? You can have a lot of movement, doing, and activity going on. You can use a lot of energy, be very committed, persistent and tenacious. The question is: What do you want to spend your energy doing? Is it enough to rake leaves, stay busy, and put on the appearance that you are accomplishing something? Or do you want to spend your energy on making a difference in your own life and in the lives of those around you?

You are given one life. You are given a calling. You have a purpose. It's up to you to choose whether or not you will take responsibility for what is yours, and use your voice, your gift, your talent--whatever it is that you've been given to bring to this planet--and use your energy to accomplish whatever it is you are here to do. It's your choice to trade in that perpetual wheel, the one that is getting you nowhere and accomplishing very little, for the path that is set before you.

Sure it's scary. It's unknown. It's risky. But is that more troubling than surviving instead of living? Is it more terrifying than getting to the end of your life and wondering who you are and if you had an impact on the world? I know it sounds dramatic, but if you dig deep down, you know that you want to do more than exist in this life. You want to make a difference, and you absolutely can. But not until you decide to step off the wheel, out of the chaos and the striving, and step onto your path.

The path won't be easy. It won't be perfect either, because you're not perfect. I'm not perfect. But you will be able to see growth and progress and your light will begin to shine to those around you. Whether you are the one to change the world, or you are the one to change the one who will change the world, you have to do it!

Get off that wheel! Get onto the path! Start living the life you were created to live! Let's get started!

CHOICE.

MAKE A DECISION NOW TO CHANGE YOUR LIFE.

WHAT DO YOU WANT?

FIND YOUR PATH AND FOLLOW IT. NO MORE EXCUSES.

Chapter 4

Yards and Fences

You must take personal responsibility. You cannot change the circumstances, the seasons, or the wind, but you can change yourself. That is something you have charge of. -Jim Rohn

So what is this "path"?

It's the path of setting limits.
It's the path of taking your power back.
It's the path of figuring out what you have control over in your life and spending your energy on those things.
It's a journey from chaos to surety and serenity.
It's how you move from frantic to grounded.
And the key is learning what it means to set healthy boundaries in your life.

You may be asking yourself, "What in the world is a boundary?" Here is an analogy that describes boundaries better than anything else I've come across.

Houses and Yards

Picture with me if you will a house. It can be the house that you live in currently, your favorite childhood home, or perhaps the dream house you hope to have in the future. Now picture the yard. The yard has a fence around it. This is your house. This is your yard. The fence tells you exactly what is yours and what is not yours. It tells you where your property begins and ends. It makes it clear what you are responsible for, and what is not your responsibility.

You can do whatever you want with your house and your yard. What color do you want to paint your house? What kind of flowers and trees do you want to plant? How often do you want to mow your grass? Who do you want to have over for a barbecue? Who do you want to entertain in your house and in your yard? These are all the choices you get to make being the homeowner. This is your yard, your house, and it is your responsibility to take care of it.

Now look next door. Picture your neighbor's house. Picture their yard. Just as you are responsible for your house and your yard, your neighbor is responsible for their house and their yard. They can paint it whatever color they want (depending on the homeowner's association rules!) They can plant whatever trees and flowers they like. They can decide when they want to mow their grass. They can entertain whoever they want to in their house and in their yard. They get to make the same choices about their property that you do about yours, and they don't need your approval to do it. You don't even have to like what they are doing in their yard, because it's not yours.

The good news is you are also not responsible for their yard, their lawn, their house, and ultimately their life. What a relief! However, sometimes you want to have more control over what they're doing. Maybe they wait 3 days longer to mow than you would. Maybe they have people over that you don't approve of. And it's ok. It's not your responsibility, your problem, or your choice. As much as you might not want to hear this, it's none of your business. More good news: What you do with your house and your yard is none of theirs either! We are all responsible for our own yard.

Gates. Every fence has a gate. You have to have one in order to get in and out, and in order to let others in and out. The best part is you are the gatekeeper! You get to decide who and what comes into your yard. You get to decide who and what doesn't get to come into your yard. You are in control of what happens in your yard. You can let the good in. You can keep the bad out. You get to decide. Isn't that empowering?

Fences Not Walls. Fences are very different than walls. Walls serve an important purpose when used correctly. They provide privacy, protection, and many other important things. As good as walls are, they are not always the best choice for boundaries. You see, walls may protect, but they also isolate and cut off. It's important for your boundaries to be more like fences, which are permeable and moveable. Fences create limits, and yet they don't disconnect you from others. Relationship and connection is important. Fences provide a way for you to have healthy ones.

What is the Purpose of Building Fences?

It's a lot easier to see and understand a boundary when it is tangible. When you see a yard with a fence and a gate, you know that it means it is someone else's property. When you are in our own yard, behind your fence, you know that you are on your own turf, and you are responsible for everything in there.

Emotional Property Lines. What is the purpose of setting boundaries and drawing these lines when it comes to your life? Just like building a fence accomplishes several things for you in the physical world, setting limits in your life and in the emotional realm serves a vital purpose as well.

Clarity. You build a fence around your physical yard because you want those around you to be clear about who it belongs to. It helps you to know exactly what you need to be responsible for, and it holds you accountable to do that. It also makes it clear what is your neighbor's property. Therefore, what they are obligated to take care of. This helps everyone to know who needs to deal with what when there is an issue. The same goes for your life. Clarity about what is mine to take care of and what is yours to take care of is crucial.

Protection. You build a fence because it gives you protection. It gives you security to know that you get to decide what and who you do and do not want within your yard. You have a choice what and who you let onto your property! Of course, you can't ultimately control it if someone opens the gate and comes into your yard, or attempts to break into your home, but you have made it clear that it is yours. You can definitely have consequences for people who deliberately trespass onto your property. The same is true in life. If someone insists on not respecting your limits, there are many ways to implement consequences to stop the behavior or else remove them from your life.

Communication. A fence also makes a statement to those around you that you have definite limits. It communicates that others need permission to enter your yard and your life, and that you have expectations of how they will behave when they are there. Some examples of those expectations are: respect, non-abusive behavior, everyone being responsible for their own self and their own "work" (personal growth and development). Once again, you cannot actually control someone else's behavior, but you can definitely decide if you will allow them to remain in your yard or in your life if they choose not to honor the "rules of the house".

Inside the Fence

How can you apply the tangible illustration of the yard and the fence to the intangible parts of your life so you can understand and be sure of what is yours to care for? Although it's hard to have an all-inclusive list, most of the things you are responsible for will fall under one of the following items:

My feelings

My attitudes

My treatment of others

My behaviors

My choices

Setting and enforcing limits

What has been given to me by God (possessions, talents, gifts)

What I want

Creating my life

Knowing what I value and believe in

Getting my needs met

My self-talk

My level of openness

Likewise, you are NOT responsible to take care of these things FOR anyone else.

Trauma and Abuse

Sometimes in the cases of abuse and trauma, it may be necessary to put up a wall. Total separation and impermeable protection may be necessary at least for a time when you are dealing with someone who has been abusive to you in the past. Sometimes it may be just a temporary wall, but there are occasions where it may be necessary to cut someone off permanently. You should not ever continue to subject yourself to abuse or mistreatment. Relationships that are toxic and sacrifice a person's well-being need to come to an end. How to deal with trauma and how it affects boundary-setting will be covered in a later chapter.

What About Helping?

Some of you caring types may be experiencing a sort of conundrum over the whole responsibility issue. When you are in relationships with people, there will be times when they legitimately need help. We all have times of crisis and trauma in our lives where we really need a helping hand. Part of being in connection and being a good friend or family member to others is being willing to pick up part of the slack when someone is truly overwhelmed and unable to do it all on their own.

This is much different than taking responsibility for something that someone needs to take care of themselves. We all have things in our lives that are challenging. We've all figured out by now that life is not easy, and sometimes we just have to plug our nose and plow through it. It is reassuring to know that the ones we love are there for us to lean on in a bind. However, as much as you think you are being helpful, it is not helping if you are rescuing someone from their own consequences or responsibility. This is actually very disempowering and debilitating to a person. We have all had times in our lives when we didn't know if we would survive, and yet we did, and now we can look back with pride and realize that we were much more resourceful and resilient than we imagined.

What is My Responsibility?

You do have responsibility TO others. You should definitely love, support, encourage and believe in those you are in relationship with. Just remember that you should not take responsibility FOR someone else's choices, behavior, or well-being. Every choice that you make and that those around you make has a consequence, either positive or negative. To get in the way of that natural process is to get in the way of them learning, growing, and being a responsible adult. If you are suffering the consequences of someone else's behavior, you are more than likely overstepping the line between being responsible TO and being responsible FOR.

Dealing with Legitimate Need

Sometimes you will encounter a person who truly is in need and cannot help themselves, or at least they can't do it alone. You are not going to be able to help everyone who is in legitimate need, even if you really want to. There are times that you are put in someone's path to be light and help to them. This is what I call being "the one". You are the one to help, to hold up, to reach out, and you should. However, this is not always the case.

Sometimes, because of lack of time, energy or resources, it may not be possible or a good time for you to help. In this situation, you need to ask yourself, "Am I able to give without putting myself in a bad position?" Am I "the one" who is supposed to help in this situation and at this time? If the answer is no, it's okay. That just means that there is someone else who likely is "the one" to help this time.

Helping Donna

I remember a time about 20 years ago when I knew I was "the one" to come alongside a friend who was going through a very dark season in her life. Donna was a single woman in one of the churches my husband was pastoring. We had become quite fond of each other and I loved her like family. She came to our house on holidays, and basically adopted all of us as her own since she had no children or grandchildren.

Donna lived with her sister, Margaret, who was also single, and they were extremely close. Her sister was quite a bit older than she was. One day I got a phone call, and Donna let me know her sister was very ill and not doing well. She had many health issues over the years, and now she had suddenly become very sick and the prognosis was not good. I spent a lot of time going over to check on my friend and her sister. Margaret began to decline rapidly. This was devastating for Donna because this was the only sibling she had left, and she had no family of her own.

I remember the day that her sister was admitted to the hospital. She had lost a lot of weight in a short amount of time, and she wasn't doing well at all. The doctors agreed to try a few things, but they were not very optimistic about Margaret getting a lot better. Donna was heart-broken. I spent many hours in the hospital waiting room holding her hand and hugging her while she cried and wondered how she would ever make it without her beloved companion. There was not much that I could do. I couldn't make it better. I couldn't give her false hope. But I was there, and it gave Donna at least a little comfort and the reassurance that she was not alone. Only a couple of days went by before the few family members and friends that Donna had left were called to come and say their goodbyes to Margaret.

We were told it wouldn't be long before her heart would give out. I spent 36 hours straight at the hospital and running errands for family. Another mutual friend and I brought food in for the family, who was very reluctant to leave Margaret's side. At this point she was in a coma and not responding to anyone, so we knew the time was near. I remember my sweet friend asking if I would sing some of the old hymns that her sister loved so much in order to give her some comfort and help her know that we were there. What an honor to be there as my friend's sister took her last breath and went to heaven. I knew that I was there for that time, and Donna was forever grateful and we had an even stronger bond that before.

I had the time to sit with her for those few days. My husband watched our children. I was working at the church helping him, and he could get along without me temporarily. I had the energy because I was in my 20's, and I knew it was temporary. I had the resources because it required me being there, being supportive and loving on my friend, which was easy for me. I was "the one" to be there for her.

A Different Time

Fast forward to 12 years later, when my husband was not in a good place physically and mentally, my daughter was struggling with depression and anxiety and not able to function at school, and my own health was suffering because of a diagnosis of fibromyalgia, I would not have been "the one". My time was consumed with making sure that my family members were okay and where they needed to be. My energy was drained because of the chaos and stress that was required when you deal with mental illness, not to mention the debilitating fatigue that comes along with fibromyalgia. Resources were lacking. I could barely hold my own life together and do everything that was required to keep everyone else functioning and safe. It was not my time to be "the one" for anyone else. As much as this was hard for me and I longed to help others, I had to focus on myself and my family. It's just the way it was at that point in my life.

What's Right for You?

There are many things that can affect your ability to help others, and I want you to know that it's okay. Depending on what season of life you are in--your health or your responsibilities--you may or may not be able to help someone in genuine need. When I feel unsure of whether or not I should be compelled to help, it's essential to ask myself if it's realistic and doable. Ask yourself: Do I have the time? Do I have the energy? Do I have the resources? This can help you to discern what is best for you and for those you care about.

I love the quote by David Allen, "You can do anything, but not everything." Such a good point! You CAN always be the one to help, but at what price? Something to think about.

> **EVALUATE.**
>
> YOU NEED TO SAY "NO" TO SOMEONE WHO IS IN LEGITIMATE NEED. YOU DO NOT HAVE THE TIME, ENERGY, OR RESOURCES RIGHT NOW.

Chapter 5

The Shadow Sides of Yes and No

Respecting the opinions and beliefs of another, even if they differ from yours, is a genuine sign of love." – Charles F. Glassman

Anytime you go to an extreme with anything, it's probably not a good thing, even if it started with the best intentions. Most things in life, however noble and positive they seem, can become distorted and out of balance. This is sometimes referred to in psychology and personal development as the "shadow" or the "shadow side" of something. The old saying that says "too much of a good thing" can definitely be true. This is also the case when we talk about saying yes and no. These can both be good when used appropriately, and they can also be taken too far. Let me give some examples.

Have you ever tasted a dessert that just wasn't quite sweet enough? It looked so good, but as soon as you put it in your mouth you realized it just wasn't quite right. I love to cook and bake, and I think I'm pretty proficient at it, but I remember one time when I was either distracted or in a hurry that I accidentally used salt instead of sugar. Wow, that was quite a shock. It looked so delicious, but the taste told the truth! My goal was to make something beautiful and tasty, and my intentions were good, but the result was not at all what I wanted it to be. My creation was a disaster.

Another great example of good intentions going wrong would be with your children. Sometimes you just want your kids to have it better than you did. You want to save them from hurts that you had. You don't want them to be "without" like you were. You want them to have more opportunities and a better life than you did. Those are normal and fine things to want for your kids, right? What parent doesn't want their kids to have every chance for the things they missed out on? However, we have all either experienced first-hand or watched people we know pay the price for overindulging their children. What started out as a wish to give them the best turns them into spoiled, entitled and ungrateful human beings. Sometimes this is even carried into adulthood. Not a pretty picture!

This principle applies to how you handle your life as well. You tend to have a mode of operation that you use, and there are definitely payoffs and challenges that go along with it. In order to make this easy to understand and for you to be able to identify where you are at in your coping with life, I'm going to use some "titles" and illustrate some behaviors. It's important to realize that while most people will identify with one or two behavior types, you may see yourself in all of them at least to some extent. I have found in my years of working with people, they generally have one predominant role and one secondary role that they operate in most of the time. The one you identify with isn't nearly as important as figuring out what is not serving you well, so try not to get too caught up in "which one" you are. This is just a tool to help you become aware of what might not be working so that you can make adjustments that will serve you much better.

The "Pleaser"

Jennifer is a 35-year-old woman who is well-liked by everyone. She is often described as sweet, loyal, and kind which makes her a great friend. She is someone that people know they can depend on to show up when they need help or a listening ear. You could definitely refer to her as a "lover not a fighter," which makes her very easy to be around. Her goal is to make sure everyone is happy and gets their needs met, and she does whatever is necessary to "keep the peace." Sound familiar to anyone?

You may be thinking, "She sounds like a pretty good person, so what's the problem?" The goal is for us to be kind and giving and look for ways to help others, right? It also seems like avoiding conflict and getting along would make life a lot easier as well.

Why Pleasing Doesn't Work

Jennifer doesn't say "No" to others. Since she doesn't say "No" to others, she doesn't say "Yes" to herself, and the result is that she is suffering, physically, emotionally, and mentally. She cannot even imagine herself saying "No" to anyone, because that seems mean and uncaring, but she says "No" to her own needs and "No" to expressing what she thinks and what she wants. She is always meeting the needs of everyone around her and playing the role that works best with everyone she is in relationship with. The question is: How long will Jennifer be able to sustain this? She may be able to do it for a while, maybe even for a long time, but one day she just won't be able to do it anymore. One day, it will become too much, and she will snap. It happens all the time. Maybe it's happened to you. I told you how it happened to me. Maybe you know someone who seemed fine, and then one day they just lost it. We give and we give and we give until the bucket runs dry. It works, until it doesn't. Eventually it all catches up with a person, and something has to change.

Jennifer appears to be sweet and kind on the outside, but what's happening on the inside is a very different scenario. She is sad. Depressed. She doesn't really know who she is or what she wants, and neither does anyone else, even those that are the closest to her. She has a lot of guilty feelings when she's not making everyone else happy and their lives easier. Yet, she doesn't even see that she is totally neglecting her own well-being.

Jennifer takes responsibility for other people's choices, and because of that, she suffers the consequences of their behavior, and they don't. She is resentful toward others for taking advantage, and even more toward herself for letting it happen, and yet she doesn't know how to change it. She's exhausted from giving so much for so long, and yet she doesn't even know how to ask to get her own needs met. She's codependent, so she rescues and enables people and thinks she's "helping." She never feels like she does enough, and the demands seem to get greater by the day.

Perhaps the saddest part about being a Pleaser is you don't see your own value. Pleasers do what they do because they have huge hearts. They really long to make a difference in the world, but they think the only way to do that is to sacrifice, give, and serve even when it costs them everything.

You are also not sure that anyone cares about or wants to know what you think or feel, so you keep it hidden deep inside. You believe that the only way to have meaningful relationships is to give other people significance and make sure you are happy. There is nothing wrong with wanting to uplift and support others, but don't forget is that it's equally as important to be the one who receives sometimes.

I am speaking from personal experience. I was that one who pleased until I just couldn't do it anymore. Sometimes I need to speak my truth. Sometimes people will not like or understand what I feel or have to say; and that's okay. It is only when I realized that sometimes my helping wasn't helping, sometimes my giving was costing me way too much, and that doing things because of the wrong motives got me the opposite of what I wanted that I started to learn how to relate in a way that respects others but also respects me. What an epiphany!

Why People Are Pleasers

There can be many reasons why you do the things you do. Most psychologists agree that there are a few things that contribute to people becoming people-pleasers or codependent: fear of failure, fear of abandonment, or fear of rejection. If you are not this type of person, you may not even understand this, but pleasers are very debilitated, paralyzed, and terrified at the thought of not making people happy that they are in relationship with. Wow, that's a pretty big task, especially considering the fact that it is not really possible to MAKE someone else happy. No wonder people-pleasers are always exhausted, frustrated, and feeling like they just can't do enough.

People-pleasing often stems from childhood issues such as:

Receiving love on a conditional basis.
Having one or both parents that were unavailable either physically or emotionally.
Severe punishment.
A parent or parents that were highly critical, rigid and hard to please.

The Eluder

Bill is a 52-year-old man who will avoid conflict at any cost. His goal in life, whether he knows it or not, is to distance himself as quickly as possible, whether physically or emotionally from anything that is uncomfortable or threatening to the shell he has built around him. He cares about people. He wants relationships. He wants connection, but others can only come so close, and he will only go so deep. Bill truly loves his wife and his children, but being vulnerable is just far too great a risk. He wants them to be happy, but he doesn't know how to accomplish satisfying relationships with his family or even his friends without letting down his guard and having to show emotion or talk about difficult things.

Why Eluding Doesn't Work

Bill never says yes to help. In fact, he will not even ask for help. He's very willing to help in solving the problems of family members, as long as it doesn't involve anything emotional, but he definitely has no interest or intention of asking for feedback and input to help solve his own personal issues. He does not feel comfortable opening up about feelings. In fact, he denies or ignores his own emotions. He also does not feel the need to build an emotional support system. He tends to minimize his problems and thinks he should be able to figure everything out on his own. He is uncomfortable dealing with feelings whether his own or others. Because of that, he doesn't always recognize emotional cues, and he has difficulty showing empathy.

Bill doesn't understand why his wife gets so frustrated with him and why he feels so disconnected from his children. He doesn't even realize the great lengths he is going to in order to deflect attention away from himself, and away from difficult conversations. He just knows that when he starts to feel uncomfortable or vulnerable, the only thing to do is to change the subject or walk away. His intention is merely to avoid conflict, but it is perceived by his family as aloof and uncaring. They feel dismissed, and even though he doesn't mean to, his avoidance causes them to feel invalidated and devalued.

Here is an example of a conversation Bill had with his wife early on in their marriage:

Jackie: "Bill, you seem like something is bothering you."

Bill: "No, I'm fine."

Jackie: "Are you sure? You seem very preoccupied and anxious about something."

Bill: "There's nothing wrong."

Jackie: "Okay, I just want you to know that I want to support you if you need to talk about anything."

Bill: (frustrated) "Why do you keep asking me if something is wrong? There's nothing wrong, except that now I'm angry because you keep asking me. Besides, if there was anything wrong, it wouldn't help to talk about it because there's nothing anyone can do anyway."

Jackie: "Well, I'm sorry for caring. I just thought it might help for you to have someone to talk to and see if we could come up with a solution."

Bill: (walks away frustrated at the intrusion)

Jackie: (walks away frustrated at the disconnection)

The pain points for the person who chooses this mode of operation are isolation, being misunderstood, disconnected from others, even though that is not what they want, loneliness, detachment, narrow perspective, frustration that they have to do everything for themselves, even though this is what they have created.

Why People Are Eluders

There are several reasons why people use avoidance as their primary coping method:

Some did not have their emotional needs met as infants or children; for example, nurturing, holding, comforting when they were hurt or afraid.

Some may have been told it's selfish to ask for what they need, that they needed to "figure it out".

Some did not have their feelings recognized or validated as a child. Maybe they were told to "stop crying" or to "deal with it."

The Eluder has carried their attachment issues into their adult relationships. They tend to have a fairly positive self-image, and they can be fiercely independent because they have learned to pull themselves up by their own bootstraps. They find safety in only relying on themselves. They tend to have a negative image of others, which is why they find it hard to make commitments. They perceive that no one else can be trusted or depended on, so it makes sense to them to give cautiously and not take or expect anything from others.

The Bully

Monica is a 41-year-old woman with a great career. She is driven, ambitious and hard-working. Monica gets what she wants in life, and is willing to do just about whatever she has to, including stepping on a few toes if necessary. It's an advantage to have her on your team at work or in life, just don't get crossways with her. She has very specific ideas about how things should be and how people she is in relationship with should operate. She is quick to let you know if you step outside of her idea of what things should look like.

She cares about the people in her life, but that can be quickly overshadowed by anger, frustration, and her need to control her own life and everything around her. The people around her, including her husband, children, friends, and co-workers find her to be abrasive and intimidating. They know they can depend on her to get things done, but they also know that there is a high cost if you get in her way or have an opinion that differs from hers.

Why Overt Controlling Doesn't Work

Monica doesn't accept "no" from others. She uses intimidation, punishment, guilt, and abuse to make sure things always go her way. She is not very good at respecting other people's ideas, choices, or limits. She isn't great at listening, validating, and accepting others as they are. This is because she believes that she knows best and that she is always right. It comes down to convincing or coercing others into seeing or doing it her way--the right way. It takes a very secure and grounded person to stand up to her because the cost is so high if you do. A person like Monica is a Bully, and they continue with their behavior for one reason, because it gets them what they want.

Although most of the pain caused by this personality is suffered by everyone they are surrounded by, there are some things that are uncomfortable for the bully even though their behavior continues to get them what they want most of the time. The Bully doesn't truly feel loved. Most people who are highly controlling realize on some level that bullying and love really can't live together.

The trouble with being a Bully is that it is a vicious cycle of narcissism, false reality, abusive behavior, false sense of rightness, entitlement, and saddest of all, it holds people at bay because they just aren't emotionally safe for others.

Why People Bully

People choose this as their way to get what they want because it works. They usually get their way because it's not worth it to stand up to them and suffer the abuse that ensues. People are intimidated by aggressive behavior, so they usually will comply in order to avoid conflict.

Where does this come from? Fear. The person fears abandonment or losing control, so they ante up their controlling behavior. This can be caused by traumatic events in childhood such as abuse (physical, emotional, mental, sexual, or spiritual), extremely controlling parents, or extremely permissive parents (leading to lack of discipline, not teaching coping and life skills and entitlement).

Abuse causes the child to feel helpless and vulnerable, and control is a way of taking their power back, albeit in a negative way. When a child is controlled and grows up in an extremely rigid and hostile environment, they learn to do the same to control others in their own lives as children and on into adulthood. When they are raised by overly permissive parents, they grow up with a sense of entitlement, no responsibility, no realization that you have to consider others and come to compromises sometimes, and they lack the discipline of being able to have feelings without acting out and taking them out on others. People who are Bullies do not take responsibility for their own behavior, and they believe that someone else is always to blame for things not working in their own lives.

The Manipulator

Craig is a 68-year-old man nearing retirement. He is always well-dressed and seems to have his life under control and keeps his emotions intact. He has been respected and well-liked by most of the people in his life because he is dependable and disciplined. You really don't notice the "shadow side" of Craig unless you have made your way into his inner circle. Once you are there, as a family member, close friend, or work closely with him on a cause or project, you begin to realize that there is more to him than meets the eye.

Craig appears to be a pretty optimistic and supportive person. He is friendly, well-groomed, and pretty easy to get along with. What people find out eventually is that even though he is not a Bully, it is still not a pleasant or desirable thing to be at odds with him. His way of "influencing" is Manipulating, which is another form of control. His approach, however, is very different than the up front, intimidating approach used by the Bully. He has a subtle way of making things go his way--the "back door approach". This can be even more disturbing than the approach of the aggressive controller, because it is very confusing and harder to recognize for what it is. Although I do not like people who are mean and overly domineering, I believe in "Say what you mean, and mean what you say," so that I at least know where I stand with someone.

Craig uses manipulation and guilt as the primary tools to get things to work out in his favor. He makes passive-aggressive comments and uses weird energy to cause people to question what they were once pretty clear about. He gives "gifts," but receiver beware, there are almost always expectations or strings attached. He definitely will keep a record, including things others do (negatively) that give him leverage, or things he has done (positively) to encourage support for his ideas and causes.

Craig also uses what I call "spiritual abuse." Spiritual abuse is: "The use of faith, belief or spiritual practices to coerce or control another person" or "coercing people into questioning themselves and going along with what the abuser wants." He uses the "God card" to coerce people into questioning themselves and their actions.

Some examples of spiritual abuse would be:

Forcing reconciliation (instead of encouraging forgiveness) between a victim and their offender.

Influencing personal decisions such as marriage, divorce, parenting.

Dictating political views.

Forcing agreement on doctrinal issues.

Forcing total submission to and agreement with spiritual authority by using shame and guilt messages (accept and don't question religious authority).

Placing more importance on outward performance than on spiritual authenticity.

Legalism (focusing on stringent rules instead of a relationship with God that offers grace). This is one of the most heinous ways that people who manipulate operate. It is wrong on every level, and it is not at all approved by God.

Why Covert Controlling Doesn't Work

As with the Bully, Craig does not accept "no" from others. The difference is that instead of being out in the open with his control, he has a much more covert approach. Once again he has learned that his behavior usually gets him to his desired outcome, so it is worth it to continue in this manner. However, there is a down side, whether he realizes it or not.

Although the Manipulator may get what they want, it is definitely through coercion and not because they have worked toward a common goal and been an influencer with a positive impact on someone else. They suffer from a lot of insecurity, which is why they feel that passive-aggressive behavior is the only way for them to get the desired outcome. Even though it may seem as though this is working, it eventually erodes relationships because people get tired of being taken advantage of and not feeling like they are respected or listened to.

The Manipulator definitely comes from a scarcity mentality. Somehow they have come to believe that there is only so much to go around, and that there isn't enough for everyone to be fulfilled and content. Otherwise, why would they insist on such tactics to make sure they always get their own way? This also contributes to them never being satisfied. After all, how fulfilling is it to get what you want if you have to do it in an underhanded and negative way?

The other pain point in this character issue is that because they don't feel safe being vulnerable (after all, they could be exposed and what they have built could immediately be dismantled). They also do not have the ability to connect on a deep level. Even if they do have a connection, they sabotage the relationship eventually because no one wants to feel like they are being coerced and guilted into doing what someone else wants when it's not of mutual benefit.

Why People Manipulate

What are some of the common reasons why people tend to be manipulators? As children, it is likely:

They did not feel like there was much value given to basic needs and wants.

They were told that they were too demanding, or they felt that they were an inconvenience to their parents.

They were made to feel like they didn't deserve whatever it was they were asking for.

It was not acceptable for them to show negative emotion—anger or sadness--and if they did, there was shame attached to it.

They were criticized, attacked, or ridiculed for asserting themselves or expressing their feelings.

If they dared to share what was really going on, they were labeled as selfish, or bad or out of control.

Thus when expression is not encouraged, repression is the only alternative. The problem with repression is that the feeling or need still persists even if it is stuffed away. You can only shove something down for so long before it starts to bubble up; resulting in passive-aggressive behavior, psychological issues, physical manifestations, etc.

The Loner

Vicki is a 57-year-old woman who has never married. She gets along fine with people at work, and has a few people that she would call "friends," but her relationships don't go beyond a superficial level. She often wonders if she should have paid more attention and pursued more intimate relationships when she was younger, since most of the people she knows have families with children and grandchildren. She doesn't think about it too much, but instead buries herself in her work and in her own interests. She is quite comfortable living a life of solitude, because she doesn't have responsibilities that keep her tied down or that require her attention. It actually seems to bother everyone else in her life that she never found "the One" or settled down and had children more than it bothers her.

Vicki is not attached intimately to anyone in her life including her family of origin. She thinks about what it would be like to have those connections like many of her coworkers and acquaintances have, but she just figures it wasn't meant to be. She realizes she didn't have the best childhood, but she is convinced that she really has nothing to complain about. After all, she had a roof over her head, clothes to wear, and she never went hungry. She has pretty much resolved herself to the fact that she wasn't meant to marry or have children or even have deep connections. She really is okay with just being kind to people, but not having to get caught up in anyone else's drama.

Vicki has a hard time tolerating anyone sharing negative feelings or dealing with any relationship issues in their lives. She is definitely not the person to call when you're having a bad day, because she doesn't really have a lot of empathy for others. In her words, she's just not "the compassionate type." She's always had the mindset that everyone should deal with their own issues. She has kind of a "buck up buttercup" approach. After all, she doesn't burden others with her problems, so they shouldn't expect her to support them emotionally. In her mind she isn't being insensitive, this is just the way it is. As that famous quote says, "If it is to be, it's up to me."- William H. Johnsen

Why Isolating Doesn't Work

Monica doesn't say "yes" to others. She doesn't see the need to be emotionally connected. The uniqueness of this personality characteristic is that the Monica may not even realize what she's missing out on. It may be all she's ever known, or all she's known for a long time. It probably doesn't even occur to her that she could have far more meaningful relationships because she is really not attached to anyone in her life.

It's painful to be the person who wants so much to connect and get their needs met in a relationship with the Loner personality. The thing is, this person, although they are quite detached are usually good people. They work hard. They do good things. They are not heartless, although it may appear that way. You can see a person like this and think, "Wow, there's something there worth exploring," but when you realize they don't have the ability or perhaps the desire to engage in a deeper relationship, it can seem like an insurmountable task to try to make that happen.

The only time that it might occur to this person that what they are doing isn't working is when they realize that their relationships don't last and people go away. They don't understand why the people in their lives are so frustrated with them and disappointed in their relational skills. They may actually believe that this is just "who they are," and they do not know how to be any different.

The other discomfort for this person is that because they tend to withhold love, either knowingly or not, it causes conflict in their relationships. This is the worst case scenario for them, because not only do they go to great lengths to avoid conflict, they don't have any idea what to do with it once it rears its ugly head. As you can see, this is quite a dilemma.

Why People Isolate

What would cause a person to be so shut down emotionally? Here are a few reasons:

Sometimes if a child or adult goes through a very traumatic situation, they feel that the only way to be safe is to shut down and not feel their feelings.

Sometimes as children, these people did not have their feelings acknowledged or validated, and perhaps they were even told they were selfish or crazy.

Sometimes in the case of abuse, they are threatened and made to believe that it never happened or that no one would ever believe them.

There are the extreme cases where people detach to the point of creating another reality or even another personality, resulting in an actual personality disorder, i.e., narcissistic personality disorder, dissociative disorder, depersonalization, multiple personality disorder, and many others.

When a person shuts down their own needs and feelings, it's understandable that it would be unrealistic to expect them to empathize with, validate, or encourage the sharing of others feeling and issues. Sometimes a person shuts down because they have a parent who is extremely abusive, mentally ill, or a substance abuser. They learn that the only one they can depend on is themselves, and they expect others to view life the same way.

So What's the Answer?

At this point you may be wondering, "With all the character traits and modes of operation that aren't working, is there any hope for healthy relationships to happen?" YES! The good news is that once you become aware of what's not working, you can work on getting yourself to a healthy place where things actually work quite well! That's the whole premise behind this entire concept of setting healthy limits in your life. It gives you the opportunity to get well emotionally, and it gives the people around you the opportunity to do the same, or go be dysfunctional somewhere else. Okay, that may seem a little harsh, but I think you know what I mean. After all, you have to choose for yourself how you want to live and relate to others, and they also get to choose who they are going to be in relationship with.

Isn't it great to know that you have choices? You can't control everything or everyone, but you can choose what you will subject yourself to. We will be discussing what DOES work later in the book, but for now, it's about being aware of how you operate as well as the people around you. This is the first step in making positive changes. You get to notice what isn't working so that you can work toward what does.

OPENNESS.

TAKE RESPONSIBILITY FOR SHUTTING LOVE OUT AND CREATING YOUR OWN LONELINESS.

OPEN YOUR HEART TO SAFE PEOPLE.

Chapter 6

The Truth About Fences

Requiring accountability while also extending your compassion is not the easiest course of action, but it is the most humane, and ultimately, the safest for the community. – Brene Brown

Choices and Consequences

Do you remember Newton's Third Law of Motion? "For every action, there is an equal and opposite reaction." Just as this Law is true in science, it is also true in life that for every choice there is a consequence, either positive or negative. It reminds me of a quote by the late Zig Ziglar that says, "You are free to choose, but you are not free from the consequences of your choice."

You may or may not like this concept, but it is just the way God set things up. The sooner you learn to believe this and embrace it, the more effectively things will operate in your life and in your relationships. This is the natural flow of the universe. Everyone has the free will to make their own choices. Everyone gets to live with the results of those choices. In a world that may not seem just, this actually is one of the parts that seems fair.

This "system" actually works well if it operates the way it should. You may ask, "Why wouldn't it operate the way it should?" It seems pretty straight forward and clear, but it is possible to interfere and mess it up, and here's how it happens:

When you don't allow people to take responsibility for their own choices. There can be a lot of reasons why someone does this. Maybe you are in a codependent relationship and you always pick up the slack or buffer the other person from suffering for poor choices. When this happens, you are getting in the way of the one making the choices doing their own work, and it stunts their emotional growth.

We suffer consequences for the choices of others. Sometimes a person rescues and enables in order to keep the peace or prevent another person from suffering consequences of their behavior. In this case, the person who needs to learn the lesson is not, and a pattern is being reinforced in which the inevitable is being perpetuated. This is why there are people well into their adult years who have no concept of responsibility and do not fear consequences. They have always been bailed out. This will continue until the codependent people in their lives decide to get out of the way and allow them to fall and learn. People who buffer are suffering for choices that were not even made by them, and something is wrong with that picture.

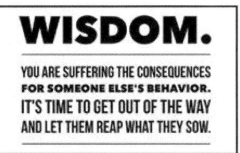

The problem with both of these scenarios is that everything works the way it should if everyone is taking responsibility for themselves. Call it reaping what you sow, call it what goes around comes around, call it if you make your bed, you also have to lie in it. The truth is that until people learn this principle, that everyone is responsible for the choices they make, and that each person gets to suffer the consequences of those choices, relationships will never be healthy and they will never work the way they were intended to. Choices and consequences are the best way we all learn and grow.

Control and Power

You cannot control everything. If you are really honest, you will realize that you actually have very little control over things and people. As we talked about in an earlier chapter, control really is an illusion. The only thing you really have control over is yourself. The good news about this is that you also have the ability to make changes within yourself.

Even though you may feel powerless at times because of your lack of control, you still have power over a lot of things. What you need to remember is that if you concentrate on using your power to change yourself and create your life, you can and will do amazing things.

In spite of all you do not have control and power over, you can actually be extremely powerful and influencing. If you will leverage the things that are within your control, and not give your power away to others, you will begin to see huge shifts in your life and relationships.

So, what do you have control over? Where does your power lie? Remember what lies within your fence? We talked in Chapter 3 about what is yours to take care of, and the great part is that these are also the things you get to be in control of and exercise your power in.

If you will truly take responsibility for what lies within your fence, you will not have time to worry about controlling other people. There's plenty here to keep you busy for a long, long time. If you will commit to mastering these things, your life will be better and you will understand what it means to be empowered.

Honor and Acceptance

Sometimes when people find out about my "Fences Not Walls" courses, they say, "What value would there be for me in taking this course. I am actually pretty good about telling others "no" and only doing things when I want to do them. What benefit is there for me?" I love it when people open up the opportunity for me to share about the "other side of the Fence."

You see, fences are not just about setting limits and making ownership clear. They aren't just about distinguishing what's mine and what's yours so that you don't get taken advantage of. They are not just about keeping people out of your yard. There is another aspect to this that some people don't think about, and maybe it's something you haven't thought about either.

Fences are not just about the yard of the neighbor building the fence. They are about all of the other neighbors understanding what a fence is for and how to be respectful of other people's property. You all understand that once a fence is built, you need permission to enter that person's yard. You expect others to understand this about your yard, but sometimes you forget that it has to be about mutual respect.

You may look over the fence and think:

"Man, when is that guy gonna mow his lawn?"

"Why is he okay letting all those weeds take over the flower beds?"

"Why does he have those kind of people over for barbecues?"

It's true that most people you know do not have exactly the same perspective about how to maintain their property as you do, but that's their business. It may be annoying or perplexing or downright frustrating to you, but it doesn't mean you can walk in their yard, mow their lawn, pull their weeds and tell their company to go home, no matter how much you want to.

It's the same way in life. Just because someone is not making the choices you would make, doing the things you think they should do, or you want them to do, just because they are not caving in to how you want them to think or behave does not give you the right to knock down their fence. Regardless of your opinions or feelings, you need to honor and respect what they have decided is best for their lives. Period.

What is the value of understanding fences and limits? It's important for you to realize if you are trespassing, and if you are, to realize and that you need to stop. If you want respect from others and for them to "mind their own business" then you need to do the same. This is not easy, however, it will build intimacy and connection in your relationships, and it's so worth it.

Intuition and Inspiration

When building fences in your life, here are two extremely important questions to consider:

What is right for me in this situation?

Why am I saying Yes or No in this situation?

Sometimes when you go to make a decision, you try to think about it, analyze it, or pick it apart. You also try to figure out the pain versus the payoff of choosing in or not. Instead of coming from your head, or from your fear, think about coming from your heart.

A lot of times when I am coaching someone and they are feeling distressed, I will ask them a question like:

"What do you think you need to do?"
"What's not working in this situation?"
"What do you think the answer is?"

The response I get often is "I don't know." I want you to know that I understand what it feels like to be in this position. I have done years of my own personal development, therapy, coaching, and sometimes it is so overwhelming that "I don't know" feels like a truthful answer.

When" I don't know" is the answer, it is because someone is overthinking or coming from a place of fear. "I don't know" feels safe in a way, and it also relieves a person from responsibility. If you don't know something, you don't have to do anything to change it. Once you "know" something, then there is an expectation that you will either stop complaining and lamenting about the situation, or you will do something to make it different.

When I or one of my clients gets stuck in the "I don't know" space, one way to get them out of it is to say, "Actually, you do know." Now, if they haven't done a lot of personal development, they may not like that statement. In fact, they don't like me sometimes, and I don't like the coaches in my life who say that to me (at least in that moment). When they begin to argue that they really don't know, it's an opportunity for me to help them find their answers. This can be done by asking more questions and getting them to tap into a different part of their brain. The most effective is when I can get someone to shift from their head and their fear into their intuition.

You know so much more than you think we do. You actually have more resources than you even realize, and they aren't "out there" somewhere. They are within you. You have a spiritual capacity inside you, whether you believe in a higher power or not. Whatever your belief is, you are a spiritual being and you have the ability to tap in to that and find direction and wisdom.

For me, that wisdom comes from God the Holy Spirit. The problem is that I get so busy. My life gets frantic. I start running on that wheel. I try to keep up by doing things that aren't working, and I lose touch with my spirit. Can you relate?

If you will get quiet, shut your brain off, breathe deeply, and ask questions, you can find your own answers. This has nothing to do with intelligence. It has to do with connecting to the Creator and listening to the direction He gives. I have experiences all the time where I don't know what to say: in a coaching session, in a class, to a grieving friend, and all of a sudden something comes to me. Something far more profound than I could ever come up with. Those are what I call "God moments", when I know I am a channel of love through which He speaks life into someone... WOW.

It's not about being brilliant. It's not about knowing more. It's not about having charisma. It's about getting quiet and reflective long enough to hear what you need to hear, and get the answers you need. And it's POWERFUL.

If you are not sure whether or not you should do something, you can tap into your soul and ask, and you will know if it is for you to do.

> **INTUITION.**
> TRUST YOURSELF. YOU WILL KNOW WHAT TO DO IF YOU GET QUIET AND **LISTEN TO YOUR HEART.**

Let's talk about Motivation. WHY you do what we do is just as important, in fact more important than WHAT you do. Most coaches, facilitators, and therapists agree that people basically are motivated by two things, Love or Fear. You cannot operate out of both of these at the same time, it's either one or the other. In Scripture there is a verse that says, "Perfect love casts out fear" which means that love and fear cannot reside together.

Make sure that whatever you are doing, whatever you are saying yes to is coming from your heart, which means it is flowing out of you because of love. Love is a much better motivator and facilitator than Fear. Fear involves words like "Could have. Should have. If only. If not." Ick! Do you see how bad that feels just energetically? Now contrast that with Love which says, "Will. Want to. Called to. Inspired to." How different does that feel?

There are times where all of us do things because we are the one who has to do them. I understand that you can't just shirk responsibility because you don't feel like being responsible. Sometimes you are not the only one who can do something. Sometimes it's okay to say no to someone else in order to say yes to something better, or to say yes to taking care of yourself. What a difference it makes when you give out of a heart full of love than out of a spirit of fear and obligation!

Assessing and Compassion

How do you go about building fences in your life? We have already discussed some of the reasons it is hard to start setting limits with people you love, and how guilty you can feel when you have to say no to people who want or need your help. It's easy to say things tritely like, "You just can't help everyone" or "You just can't worry about what people think." It's equally as important to realize the importance of setting limits that work for you while at the same time staying connected and compassionate towards those who may be affected by your fences.

There are going to be times when you want to help or give, but you're not sure if you should. I've given you a few tools that I hope will assist you in making healthy decisions about when you should or shouldn't. These are great questions to ask when someone asks for help.

Regardless of the decision you make and the direction you decide to go, you can and should always do it with compassion.

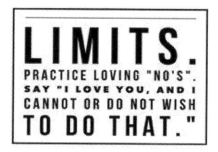

I told my kids as they were growing up that it took the same amount of energy to be kind as it did to be nasty. Nasty can actually suck energy out of you, and it definitely has a negative effect on the people around you. You should be kind, no matter what. I even think this applies when you are having hard conversations with people. You can say things with kindness and a neutral energy no matter what it is. The same is true in building fences. You can be crystal clear about your limits. You can make sure the other person understands what you are willing and not willing to do. You can even tell someone that you are choosing to not be a part of their life, and this can all be done with compassion and kindness.

The fence you build is neutral. It is not personal. It is not a weapon. It's a statement of who owns what. That's all. It really has no energy. Like we talked about before, you actually cannot insist that someone respect your boundary. Unless you have a lock on the gate, you can't really prevent someone from coming into your yard (without threatening them with force), but you can definitely follow through with the consequences you have set for such trespassing. The great part about a consequence is that you don't even have to be the bad guy! Even with kids, you can state the limit, communicate it clearly and without raising your voice, and enforce the consequence, and you make it all about their choice. Isn't it great to know that you can build fences without hostility, anger, guilt, manipulation, or nastiness?

Even if you are as kind as can be, the other person may still insist on being angry, offended, and violate the boundary anyway. So what does that tell you? You can feel good about the limit you set, why you set it, and how you went about it, because their reaction is not about you at all! So, be kind, AND do what you need to do. Make your decision with compassion, and let go of the results.

Intention and Action

Are you into the zombie movement? I was visiting my son at college awhile back, and he tried to get me to watch a series about zombies. It was just a little too far-fetched and, frankly, just creepy for me, so I didn't even make it through the first episode. However, when I started to write this section in the book, I thought it actually might be a good analogy to refer to.

I didn't watch much, but what I observed was that these creatures, who looked like people, wandered around in a stupor. I don't really know what they were driven or motivated by, but it appeared that they were just going through the motions with no awareness or emotional connection to anyone or anything around them. How is that similar to how you and I operate at times? We live our lives on autopilot, and we don't even stop to evaluate whether or not what we are doing is working or making a difference. That's why it's so important to do personal development. It's why seeing a coach and trying to get a direction is valuable and necessary. It's the reason reading self-help books like this can give us so much insight, so that we can become AWARE. Here's how I see the process:

Unaware>>>>>>Aware>>>>>>Grounded

The key is that you have to decide to become aware. It's not easy. It's kind of scary. There's something safe about being a zombie. You're numb. You don't have to do anything different. You can wander around, and say "I don't know." The thing about awareness is this: Once you KNOW, you can't go back to NOT KNOWING. Oh no! Now you have to be accountable!

The awareness phase is uncomfortable. Now you know what's not working. Now you realize that you're angry at yourself and at others because you haven't set any boundaries. It's uncomfortable, but it will get better. Eventually as you practice setting limits and building healthy relationships you will move to the final phase: Grounded.

What does Grounded look like?

Moving from making adjustments in current relationships to setting up the perimeters right from the start in new relationships.

Making your boundaries clear and following through with consequences so that people aren't confused and you aren't exhausted and resentful.

Someone who is clear about their responsibility and their calling and that realizes that everyone else is responsible for theirs. It looks like proactivity.

The only way to have the life you want is to be intentional and to choose what you want your life to look like. It's never going to happen accidentally, so what are you waiting for? Move toward awareness, on purpose, and one day you will find that you are grounded.

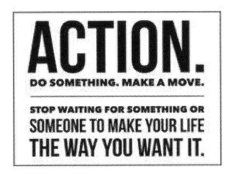

Gratitude and Stewardship

Is it okay to want something that you don't have? I think it is, and it's probably pretty normal. When is it not okay? When you move from simply noticing something that someone else has that would be nice to have, to becoming envious and obsessed, you have a problem. What is the problem with envy? You compare yourself and your life to others, you are not able to be happy for others, and it causes you to devalue what you already have.

What's the harm in comparing yourself to others? Comparing is really a form of judgement. When you compare yourself with someone, you are

Swallowed Up

not only judging them, but you are judging yourself. How many times do you think you know how someone is doing, how their life is going, or how successful they are? How do you think you know that? Usually by the way they look, or act, or talk. What if the image they portray is not an accurate representation of what's really going on? How many times have you dressed up, showed up, put a smile on and told everyone how great things were going for you, and you knew it wasn't true? Be careful about judging others by your first impression or by the outward image, because you don't know the whole story.

You also judge yourself when you compare yourself to someone else. It's really not a fair way to evaluate how you are doing and if you are successful. Why? Because you are not them. You bring unique gifts and talents to the planet, and nobody can do what you do exactly like you do. If you are comparing yourself to someone who has different strengths, different gifts, a different calling than you, you are guaranteed to be disappointed and feel like you are not enough. So stop it! It's not valuable.

Yes, have mentors. Have people you look to for guidance and expertise. Spend time with people who inspire you; but don't compare. Even if you do the same job or project or calling as someone else, it is not going to look the same, and it shouldn't! Be who you were meant to be; it will work so much better, and you will be powerful because you are striving to be the best version of yourself.

What about not being happy for others? Have you ever known someone who just couldn't celebrate with other people? No matter what good thing happens to someone else, and how hard someone else worked or how much someone else deserved success or happiness, this person just has to find something to criticize. They have to figure out why it's just not fair. How sad. How miserable it must be to not be able to share in someone else's growth or success or excitement. After all, don't you want the people in your life to be happy for you? Proud of you? Cheering for you? Celebrating with you? Of course you do! It's always more fun to have someone join you in your happiness!

People who cannot be happy for others are operating out of a scarcity mindset. Somehow they believe that if someone else gets something, then there must be less for them. What a limiting belief! There is plenty to go around. As long as you carry this scarcity mentality around with you, you will actually block abundance from coming your way. Start being happy for others and see how it shifts your mindset, your attitude, and ultimately your own success.

Ultimately envy devalues what you already have. Kind of a sobering thought, isn't it? Are there people that have more than you? Of course. Are there people that have less than you? Absolutely. If you really think about it, are you really lacking anything you need to survive? Probably not. Most of us in this country, even if we make a modest living have way more than we need. Does it mean it's not okay to want more? I don't think so. Catch yourself when you begin to go down the path of envy, and remind yourself that you are blessed.

I am not saying that some of you reading this have not been through tough times, even financially. I know I have. All I'm saying is that being envious doesn't help you get what you want at all. Why spend the energy feeling bad about someone else's life, possessions, or success? Why not put your energy into figuring out how to improve your own situation? What do I mean by that?

Well, what is it that you really want? Do something that will move you in that direction:

Take a class.

Get some coaching to work through issues holding you back in your relationships.

Quit your job that you are miserable at and do something you love, or at least something you love more than what you're doing now.

Make an effort to meet new people; people that will encourage and inspire you to become better.

Work on your spiritual life; go to church, join a small group, meditate, spend time in nature, serve.

This is called stewardship. It's about taking care of what you've been given, making the most of it, and using it to change lives. We are all here to affect each other. It's not just about you. It's about touching and changing lives.

Most importantly, be grateful. The more you acknowledge and are thankful for everything in your life, the more grateful you will feel. It's a matter of focusing on what you have. It's about knowing that you have enough, and that you are enough. Choose gratitude, and watch your life change.

You are brilliant. Yes, you. You can do things in a way that no one else can. You can reach people that others can't reach. You bring gifts to the world that it wants and needs. You are here for a reason. Stop wasting time worrying about why your life isn't like someone else's, make your own amazing life. Start now.

> **GRATITUDE.**
> YOUR ENVY ONLY DEVALUES WHAT YOU HAVE. BE GRATEFUL, AND IF YOU WANT MORE, DECIDE HOW TO MAKE IT HAPPEN.

Interruption and Changing Direction

Are you tired of the way things are going in your life? Are you stressed about the status or health of your relationships? Remember when we talked about the things that are inside your fence--the things you are responsible for? It is your responsibility to create the life you want. It is your job to use what you have been given by God, your possessions, your talents, and your abilities to live a healthy and productive life that will serve you well along with those around you.

What do you do if things just don't seem to be working? First, realize you are the only one that can really make a change. It's not going to happen just because you want it to really bad. I love fairy tales as much as the next person, but real life just doesn't work that way:

Wishing upon a star isn't going to fix it.

Waiting for your fairy godmother to show up is a waste of time.

So is waiting for your handsome prince.

It's not going to happen!

In fact, as much as I believe in prayer and that God wants the best for our lives, what I know is that He doesn't just snap his fingers and make your life different. He has given you all that you need to do what you are supposed to do. The only way things are going to change for the better is if you start moving. You're going to have to do something.

Now, if you're like me, you can really overthink this one. I can get myself so worked up over whether or not I know enough, or whether or not it's even a good idea, or thinking about what happens if I fail. It's enough to debilitate anyone. Sometimes the most important thing you can do is something different than what you've been doing. You don't have to do it perfect. It doesn't even have to work! There are no guarantees, right? What have you got to lose? What you're doing now isn't making you any progress, so you might as well try something different. Interrupt the pattern—the one you've been operating in for so long. The one that has you stuck and miserable. It can't get any worse than what it is, right? Go for it! It is okay to try and fail. It is not okay to not try at all.

Some of the most famous business people and inventors we know experienced a lot of failure. Here's a short list, and there are many, many more: Walt Disney, Oprah Winfrey, Steven Spielberg, R.H. Macy (Macy's Department Stores), Soichiro Honda, Colonel Sanders (KFC), Sir Isaac Newton, Vera Wang (designer), Thomas Edison, Sidney Poitier (actor), Albert Einstein, Fred Astaire, J.K. Rowling (Harry Potter author), Vincent Van Gogh, Harrison Ford, Dr. Suess, Lucille Ball, Winston Churchill, Henry Ford, Sir James Dyson (vacuum inventor), Stephen King, Lady Gaga, the list goes on. Read their biographies. It's amazing to see what they accomplished against all odds.

Did you know that Sir James Dyson, inventor of the famous Dyson vacuum, made 5,126 prototypes that failed? It's true. What if he would have just quit and done nothing after that? But he didn't. He made number 5,127, and he is now worth an estimated $4.9 BILLION.

These people tried a lot of things that didn't work. They bombed!! But they didn't give up. They kept trying different ways to make things work. Failure is not failure as long as you are learning. Who knows? You may be one failure away from cracking the code in whatever area in your life you want to change. Don't wait. Get busy!

Clarity and Communicating

It is important to make your boundaries clear. This may not be comfortable if you have not ever really set any, or if you are someone who has a hard time using your voice. It's uncomfortable if you have been a pleaser, avoidant, or passive aggressive in the past. These modes of operation will not work, and they definitely won't help you on your journey toward a healthy life and good relationships. It's going to take some practice, but it really is the only way for others to have the opportunity to start appreciating who you are and how to operate in a relationship with you. Why is it necessary to speak your boundaries, out loud, with clarity? Here's a few reasons:

First of all, it's what's fair to others. If you don't communicate your limits, and you build invisible fences, you are just setting the other person and your relationships up for failure. Other people can't read your mind! Even a well-intentioned person who cares about you and wants to give you consideration and respect will fall short if they don't know the rules of the game.

Have you ever tried to learn a new game, or skill, or sport, and you had someone trying to teach you that didn't do a very good job? Maybe they didn't give you all of the information. Maybe they used words you couldn't understand. Oh, and I love this one, "Just start playing, it's the best way to learn." Sometimes it's easier to learn by doing. But boundaries are not one of those things. Do you remember how frustrated you were when you didn't know what was expected? Do you remember how silly you felt when you played the way you thought it was supposed to be done and found out there were a whole bunch of instructions and rules left out? That is how others will feel about your boundaries if you don't communicate them simply and clearly.

Others can't respect your boundaries if they are a secret. Remember when they came out quite a few years ago with the invisible fence for dogs? We all thought it was a pretty great concept. A lot of people have them, and my understanding is that they work quite well. There's just one catch, they don't work unless the dog is wearing a collar that gives them a slight shock when they try to cross the line. It's effective for dogs. People? Not so much. The fence has to be visible if it's going to work.

You will want to make your boundaries clear because others cannot help you if they don't know what you need. Remember how we talked about the fact that fences are not just about keeping people or things out that you don't want in your life? They are about preserving or keeping in the people and things you do want there. It is your responsibility not only to keep the toxic stuff out. It's your job to let in and nurture what you do want in your life. If you need or want something, try asking for it. You will not always get it, but it will definitely improve your chances. So ask. You may be surprised.

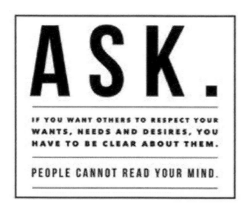

If you choose not to communicate your boundaries and make them clear to others, you really have to take responsibility for others not honoring them. How can they if they don't know? If you don't make your boundaries known, you really can't be angry if others come on your property or don't honor the rules while they are there.

You may be feeling a little overwhelmed at this point. Maybe a lot! But take heart. This is a process. It's a journey. It takes a while to process and implement these concepts, because it's so different than what you are familiar with. Stay the course. You will get it. It's about taking baby steps. Remember that you are moving from unaware-to-aware-to-grounded. Celebrate your progress. Give yourself grace. Just don't give up. You are on your way to a better life and better relationships. It will be worth it!

Swallowed Up

Chapter 7

Confusion About Fences

Setting boundaries is a way of caring for myself. It doesn't make me mean, selfish, or uncaring (just) because I don't do things your way. I care about me, too. – Christine Morgan

Are you still having a hard time translating the idea of property lines, fences and gates into your relationships? If you are, you are not alone. Hopefully now you have a little more knowledge and understanding of the importance and legitimacy of setting boundaries. You probably still have a lot of questions, fears, and misconceptions about what setting limits actually involves and what it could cost you as you begin to implement them into your life. In this chapter, we are going to address some common misbeliefs that are generally associated with what it means to set boundaries in your life. These come from common concerns, and I hope that you will be able to put to rest some of the negative connotations you have about building fences in your emotional life.

Are Fences Mean?

This is a definite concern you may have, especially if you happen to be a person who loves to give, help, and serve others. Maybe it would be helpful to replace the word "boundaries" with "fences" in order to see that they are actually more neutral and helpful than they sound.

So, if I asked you, "Are fences mean?" You would probably laugh and say, "No, that's ridiculous! How can a fence be mean? A fence is not alive. It's just a barrier put in place so that I know what is my yard and what is not. It tells me what I am responsible for and what I am not. It gives me the opportunity to create the kind of yard and garden and atmosphere that I want. No, it's not mean, a fence is a good thing!"

Maybe you wouldn't use those words exactly, but I think you get the idea.

What about the emotional fences you build in your life? What about the property lines that help you to know where you begin and end, and where the next person begins and ends? Are those mean? Of course not! In fact, they are important, and they are actually necessary.

Now, will people get offended, hurt or angry about you building fences in your life? Possibly. Does that mean you shouldn't build them? Absolutely not! Remember that you have been operating without setting limits in your life for a long time, so when you change things, it's going to be uncomfortable. It will be for you, and it definitely will be for others. When you start being responsible for yourself and allowing other to take responsibility for themselves, and when you stop taking care of others in your life, and you start loving and supporting them, but refusing to get involved in what is their job, they will not like it. Notice I did not say you didn't have any responsibility in their life. Nor did I say that you shouldn't care. I said don't take responsibility FOR them and don't take care OF them. You have been saving them a lot of time, and pain, and suffering their consequences, and it's been a pretty good deal for them.

The Gift

Perhaps if you can get past the discomfort and the hurt feelings of the other person, you will realize that you are actually creating value for them. They may not see it that way, but you are actually giving them a gift. The gift that you are giving them, although it may feel mean to them and insensitive to you is the gift of believing that they are capable and competent enough to be responsible for their own life.

Think of it this way. What kid loves chores? (What adult loves chores? Ha!) What is the purpose of assigning chores to a child?

    1) To teach them how to function in the world.
    2) To show them how to be grateful for what they have.

3) To give them a sense of how to be a contributing member of the team (family).

4) To show them how to be good stewards of what they have.

These are just a few, but you know how important these life lessons can be. You also realize that these things cannot be learned if you take over and do them yourself. It may seem easier at the time, but you will be creating a lazy, irresponsible, entitled human being who will be totally dysfunctional when they go out on their own.

You are not being mean, you are giving them the gift of stewardship, the opportunity to pull their own weight, and to reap the benefits of doing that, which are: self-esteem, confidence in their abilities, relationships skills, gratitude. Do you see how that changes the whole perception of "giving chores"? It may not feel good to them or to you. But it is truly what's best for everyone involved, and it is what's healthy in the long run. The same goes for allowing people to be responsible for their own lives. Think of it as empowering them.

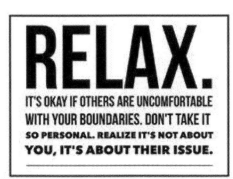

Are Fences Selfish?

I'm guessing that most parents bring up their kids to be kind to others. I know I was brought up that way. I remember:

Being taught to share.

Being encouraged to give, even sacrificially.

Being told to put others first.

I actually believe that these are all good things. They are things I taught my own children, and I try to live my life this way to this day. The problem is when things get way out of balance.

For some reason, I embraced some very distorted thinking along the way. I realize now that I had the belief (whether it was taught to me or I just interpreted it this way) that it was neither good nor acceptable to be concerned about what I wanted or needed. Somehow I came to the conclusion that it was actually selfish or wrong to say what I wanted, or to think about what I needed rather than focusing on giving to and serving others.

Anything taken to an extreme is harmful. If I only care about myself and my needs, I become narcissistic and entitled. Yet, if I only care about doing for others I can get exhausted, depleted, and become a "martyr" of sorts. It's so important to realize that taking care of yourself is not selfish, it's essential. If you become burned out, or sick, or resentful for over-giving, or you ultimately die from neglecting to care for yourself, physically, emotionally mentally, or spiritually (which actually happens to people that become caregivers for others), how much do you think you will be able to give others at that point?

Imagine if you took care of everyone else's yard in your neighborhood. You mowed their lawns, trimmed their bushes, weeded their gardens, pruned their trees. Do you think you would have the time and energy to take care of your own yard? Of course not. You would be exhausted.

You would have to quit your job. Your family probably wouldn't see you very much. You would be unhappy and resentful that you didn't have time for your own yard because you were working so hard to make their yards beautiful. Kind of silly isn't it? The crazy part is, it's not really that far off from what happens to you when you neglect yourself because you are so busy running around taking care of everyone else and all of their issues. Doesn't it seem like a much better plan for everyone to take care of their own yards and lives and then help each other out if necessary? I say, "Yes".

The Gift

What is the gift you give when you practice self-love and self-care? You are just going to be a much nicer person to be around, and who doesn't want that? Think about it; if you get proper rest, feed your body at the right times with the right food, take time to be quiet and get grounded, take care of what has been given to you, how much better do you think you will feel? Physically, mentally, spiritually, emotionally? A lot better!

If this is true, then it makes sense that if you take good care of yourself, you will automatically be able to do a better job in all areas of your life, including helping and supporting others. If you are in optimal health in every way (which doesn't happen accidentally, by the way) then how much more energy, time, joy, and resources will you have to reach out to those you love and care about? I'd say those are pretty good gifts.

I know it's an illustration that has been used a lot, maybe even overused, but it is still the best description of self-care that I have heard. It has to do with the instructions that you are given when you get on a plane to go somewhere. The stewardess does her safety presentation. When she comes to the part about "in the event there is a change in cabin pressure, oxygen masks will automatically drop from above you." Then they proceed to show you how to put it on, etc. "Be sure that if you are traveling with a child that you secure your mask first before assisting the child." I remember the first time I heard that, it sounded counterintuitive. That must be why they made a point of bringing it up.

It's our natural instinct, especially as mothers, to think of our child first and be willing to sacrifice ourselves, right? However, it's the same concept as above, if you are not okay, breathing, alive, you are not going to be much good to anyone else no matter how good your intentions are. Enough said.

Are Fences Unspiritual?

If you do not have a background that was bathed in spirituality, you may not even understand. You may think, "What does being spiritual have to do with setting limits?" Well, let me give you some examples.

I remember being in 2nd grade Sunday school class, and the lesson was about loving others. This resonated with me a lot because I have always been extremely loving and relationships are so important to me. I don't remember the exact Bible story or much else about the class that day, but there is one thing that I remember vividly and that I really took to heart. The Sunday school teacher drew on the blackboard (yes, I am that old) the letters J O Y. She said, "Who can tell me what that spells?" In unison, we all chimed, "Joy!!" Then she proceeded to ask us what we thought it meant to have Joy. We took turns raising our hands and giving our answers. "Happy", "Glad", "Smiling", etc. Then she said, "Well today I'm going to tell you how you can always have Joy." We were excited! After all, who wouldn't want to know how to do that? She then wrote the letters again, but this time instead of straight across, she wrote the letters vertically and made an acronym:

J-Jesus

O-Others

Y-You

Then she told us, if you want to have joy in your life, this is how you do that; Jesus comes first, others come second, and you come last. Make sure that Jesus is number 1 in your life, then give and love and serve others, and make sure that you always put yourself last, and you will always have Joy.

Now I admit, I tend to take things very literally. I have been guilty of black and white thinking, and regardless of whether the intention of my Sunday school teacher was to convince me that it was wrong or selfish to think about myself, that is how I took it. Can you see how I equated being "spiritual" with living a life of loving sacrifices; to my Lord, and to the people around me, and how it seemed very right and good to put myself on the back burner? I don't know if my teacher actually said these words, but this is what I heard and interpreted in my young mind, "Don't worry about yourself. Love God. Love others. If you do this, you will be a happy and spiritual person."

I remember the first time I read about self-care. It seemed so wrong. It seemed so narcissistic. If I'm doing what I should; loving God and loving others, I shouldn't have to "take care of myself" because God is going to take care of me. It seems rather naïve and simplistic, but in my child's mind, it was gospel truth. You can probably imagine how disappointed I was in my 30's when I realized that I was NOT joyful and that no one was taking care of me. I was exhausted, sick, resentful, sad, and confused about why I had done what I thought was right and yet I felt so abandoned, by God, by others, and especially by myself.

I grew up hearing all the Bible stories multiple times. My goal was to be like Jesus, and I really thought that's what I was doing. After all, Jesus was always loving, caring, and healing people. He was always spending time with the broken-hearted and those who were down and out. Even in my adult mind, I don't think I thought Jesus even ate or slept. I just always pictured him as being with people, smiling, having a lot of energy, and not really needing "down time." He just gave and gave and gave and never really worried about himself, or is that really true?

I'm sure I had heard the stories about Jesus that I'm about to share at some point in my life, but for some reason, it seemed like a new one I had never heard before. I remember almost being in resistance to it because it went against the idea I had in my mind of how Jesus spent his time.

"Very early in the morning, while it was still dark, Jesus got up, left the house and went off to a solitary place, where he prayed." (Mark 1:35)

"The news about him spread all the more, so that crowds of people came to hear him and to be healed of their sicknesses. But Jesus often withdrew to lonely places and prayed." (Luke 5:15-16)

"Because so many people were coming and going that they did not even have a chance to eat, He said to His disciples, 'Come with me by yourselves to a quiet place and get some rest.' So they went away by themselves in a boat to a solitary place." (Mark 6:31-32)

Wait, what? What do you mean Jesus went off by himself? What do you mean sometimes He even took his disciples with him? What about all of those people that had desperately followed him in hopes of him touching them and healing them, or them just being grateful to be in his presence and gaining hope and encouragement? You mean He just left them all there, clamoring for his attention? Wow, that's not exactly a picture of Jesus that I felt comfortable with at all; but that's exactly what He did, and on a regular basis, apparently.

The most interesting part of this to me is that Jesus was fully aware that He would not live to be very old. Yes, He was human, but He was also God, and He understood what His purpose was. You need to make the most of every day. Time is precious, and you need to be loving those around you as much as possible since you don't know how much time you have. Jesus knew He didn't have much time on earth, and yet He also knew that it was necessary for him to have a reprieve from others and reconnect with His Father. Wow, that was a huge realization for me.

So, is a fence unspiritual? No, because a fence is not a person. It's not who you are. It's just there to make sure that you are protected and nurtured and taken care of. It was both an epiphany and a relief for me to know that it's okay for me to step back and take time to regenerate, reprioritize, reevaluate, and most importantly recharge my soul.

The Gift

Stepping back and even away from people you love, and people who legitimately need help is necessary if you want to continue to give and love and serve. In fact, it helps you to do that better and for longer. It also keeps you in balance so you don't get resentful about people wanting too much from you.

It's also a gift to yourself, because you know that it is not only helpful but necessary if you want to be in alignment spiritually that you shut out all of the noise around you. It is very hard, maybe impossible to connect in a deep way with God, your spirit, your purpose, if you are not regularly taking time to be quiet and listen for the answers and direction you so desperately need.

There was a time in my life where I was so overwhelmed. It was in the early years of beginning to understand and implement boundaries into my life, and I wasn't quite proficient at it. I was in my early 30's, and I was in a small group at church that had women of all different ages and backgrounds. I was particularly discouraged one day, and I shared how draining and frustrating I was finding my life to be. I also was battling depression which I had struggled with for many years. I knew these people loved me, and I had been with them enough to feel safe in sharing how I was struggling.

They did what most of us do, and what I know is that they had good intentions. Sometimes it is uncomfortable for us to hear that other people are hurting or struggling, and we desperately long to have an answer or solution to fix their problem. I know I have been guilty of this as well.

Many suggestions were given to me that night by these precious people that really wanted to see me break out of this dark time. "What really helps me when I'm feeling this way is to write down everything I'm grateful for," offered one woman in the group. Another friend piped in, "I think the best thing to do when you're feeling down is to do something kind for someone else." "I like to listen to worship music, it really uplifts me," was the advice from yet another. Several others thoughtfully shared things that they hoped would be helpful. More prayer. More Bible reading, volunteering, etc. While I was grateful that they cared and wanted to help, somehow, the suggestions they were giving me only made me feel more overwhelmed and guilty that I couldn't get a handle on my funkiness. Then a woman, probably in her 40's said, "You know Angie, it sounds to me like you are just exhausted. I know that when I'm just wiped out and weighted down by life that it makes me very emotional, irrational, and just blue. I'm going to say something that may sound kind of strange, and I don't know if anyone else will agree, but honestly, I think that sometimes the most spiritual thing you can do is take a nap."

Wow! I had never even considered that! But I have to admit, I liked it! She was right. I was just bone-tired and emotionally exhausted and until I got some rest, there probably wasn't anything that was going to make me feel any better no matter how spiritual it seemed! It was brilliant. It was a relief! It's something I have used in my coaching over the years.

When my world seems to be caving in on me and I can't figure out how to fix it, I will ask myself "Is this 'my tired self' talking?" If it is, I realize that the best thing for me and everyone else is to just go to bed! Fences preserve spirituality. How cool is that?

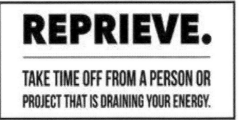

Are Fences Irresponsible?

What do I mean by this? How could setting boundaries be irresponsible? Well, if I have taken responsibility for things that others should be handling themselves, then it's possible you could FEEL irresponsible when you set boundaries and stop doing that. Is this really the reality though?

Does building a fence make you irresponsible? Or does it make everyone responsible for their own yard? Will it be comfortable or exciting for the other person if you stop taking care of their yard and concentrate on yours? Of course not. They will have to figure out how to pull their weight and do their part. It's going to be inconvenient for them to have to figure it out, because they've had a pretty good deal going.

Can you imagine how ridiculous it would be if the homeowner's association came to you and said, "We've noticed that you are no longer cleaning up and mowing all of the lawns in the neighborhood. We are not happy about this. What is causing you to shirk your responsibility in this area?" Maybe your response would be, "I realize that I have been doing everyone else's work for a long time, but I now know that I really need to concentrate on my own yard and let other people take responsibility for theirs." Who could actually argue with that? They may not be happy about it, but you absolutely cannot think that by not doing other people's jobs that you are irresponsible.

The Gift

I love the quote that says, "It is far better to do a few things well than to undertake many good works and leave them half-done." - St. Francis de Sales. The gift in being responsible for yourself and allowing other people to do the same is that you can focus on doing what you are called to do and you can do a great job at it. This reminds me of a Scripture in the Bible that says, "What good is it for someone to gain the whole world, yet forfeit their soul?" How can it be a good thing to kill yourself doing things that really are not yours to do, especially if you suffer, your family suffers, your calling suffers, and your relationships suffer?

Do you want to know how to make the biggest impact in this world? Do you want to be able to give and serve out of love and not out of exhaustion and resentment? Do your own stuff, and do it well. Be a good steward of what you've been given, because THAT is what God requires, and this my friend is the only way to experience true and lasting JOY!

Are Fences Damaging to Relationships?

I know that one of the hardest things for me to accept in setting boundaries is that the people I set limits with may feel hurt. I am a very sensitive, loving person, and one of the worst things I can think of is causing someone pain. I do not want to hurt people's feelings. Now, I'm not saying that you should just do or say whatever you want without considering other people's feelings, that definitely wouldn't be kind or right. However, sometimes when you have been getting in the way of other's suffering the natural consequences for their choices, it is possible that they will experience pain or at least a lot of discomfort when you stop doing that.

> **COMPASSION.**
> **YOUR BOUNDARY MAY CAUSE SOMEONE TO FEEL HURT.**
> **BE CONSIDERATE OF THEIR FEELINGS, BUT DO WHAT YOU KNOW YOU NEED TO DO.**

Have you ever had an injury, an illness, or a surgery that caused quite a bit of pain? Perhaps you were prescribed pain-killers to numb the pain. Do you remember how good it felt when the meds finally kicked in and you experienced relief from the pain? Did it mean that the source of the pain was gone? No, you just were not feeling the pain because the medicine was buffering it. You probably also remember what it felt like when the meds started to wear off. First it was uncomfortable, then annoying, and at some point it became downright painful again.

People who are caring can be just like those drugs used to numb pain. I know, because I did it for a long time. I buffered people I loved so that they would not experience the pain of their choices. It felt like I was loving. But the problem is, it didn't make the problems go away. It just perpetuated the inevitable. You see, pain is actually very valuable. You need to feel pain in order to know that something is wrong. If you don't feel pain, whether physically or emotionally, you continue down paths that are destructive and sometimes deadly.

Does setting boundaries mean I'm abandoning the other person? It may feel that way at first, depending on how much you have been doing for them that they should have been doing for themselves. You may be doing a lot of things for other people that God never intended for you to do. Remember how we talked about who is responsible for what? When you are in loving relationships, it is expected that you will support and encourage the other person and help them when things are too much for them to carry alone. That is not the same as enabling someone to be irresponsible and taking on for them the things that they are perfectly capable of doing for themselves.

There are several problems with doing for others what they should be doing for themselves.

You are basically saying to them, even if you don't verbalize it, that you don't think they are capable of taking care of themselves and what they have been given.

It is debilitating to people, even to your own children, if you do not step back and allow them to realize that they can figure things out for themselves. Think of it as taking their power away when you have the impulse to jump in and rescue them.

You are leaving them vulnerable and basically defenseless if something were to happen to you. It is really not helpful and loving not to give someone the tools and the opportunity to be self-sufficient, because there are no guarantees that you will be able to protect them and be there for them always. Don't you want to know that the people you love will go on to live successful, healthy, mature lives regardless of what happens to you?

What if someone else abandons me because I set boundaries? This is always a possibility. When you begin to set boundaries and start to allow others to be responsible for themselves, they may decide that they don't like the new arrangement. At this point they have two options, stay and renegotiate the relationship, or leave. You will realize that you cannot control another human being. People have choices. Healthy relationships require that both parties choose to participate in the relationship in a way that works for both. It takes two people working together to make a relationships work and last.

The truth is that setting boundaries and the other person's willingness or unwillingness to respect the boundary actually reveals the true nature of the relationship. I have always been a very compliant person whose main goal was to please and avoid conflict. I had a dear friend point out to me one time when I was dissatisfied in a relationship because I didn't feel like my wants and needs were respected, that maybe I wasn't in a "real relationship." Ouch! I admit, that didn't feel good at all, and my first reaction was to defend myself and the relationship. It didn't take me very long to realize that she had a great point. If one person in a relationship is always acquiescing to the other person, if one person is always comfortable and the other person is never comfortable, if one person always gets what they want and the other person never gets what they want, it's a very superficial and unfulfilling relationship. If there is not mutual respect, consideration and satisfaction, it's not a deep, real or sustainable arrangement.

It's terrifying to think that maybe you are in a relationship that you have convinced yourself is real and working when it actually isn't. No one wants to believe that the other person doesn't want the best for both people and that there's a possibility that they would not be willing to negotiate the terms of the relationship for the betterment of all involved, but it happens.

The Gift

It's a little trickier to find the gift in this one. But it is there. The gift that you are giving in being compassionate but building the fence anyway is this, relationships are so important. Life is too short to pretend, compromise, put up with, settle for, or get stuck in relationships that aren't real and that don't support you in your life and in your purpose. Better to find out now if the people in your life are there because they love and value you, or if you are just a convenience for them.

You need to have people in your life that you give to without expecting anything in return. This is called service. By the same token, every relationship in your life cannot be like that. You need support. You need love. You need respect. These are not too much to ask for, and you need to find people who can provide those things for you. The gift is that you are not going to lie to yourself or those around you about the nature of your relationships any more. Let go of what no longer serves you, and make room for what will. It's not going to be easy, but it will be worth it.

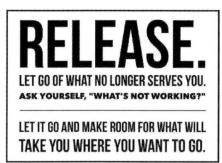

Are Fences Limiting to Others and Myself?

Sometimes it's easy to believe that "no" is always a restrictive and limiting answer. You think, "What if I miss out on something? What if there's nobody else to take that project on? What if that person can't find anyone else to help, then what? A lot of times you say "yes" out of fear that somehow you are limiting possibilities. May I suggest a different perspective here? What if your saying "no" is actually what will help you and others to expand? "How is that possible?" you may ask. Well, let's explore this a little bit.

I am a firm believer in timing. It totally makes sense to me that the right thing at the wrong time is the wrong thing. Let's take planting flowers for example. Planting flowers is a great thing, right? It makes things beautiful and bright. It makes people happy. What could possibly be wrong with planting flowers? There is a right and a wrong time to plant flowers. When you plant flowers is not a moral issue, that's ridiculous. If you plant flowers in the middle of the winter, you're going to be very disappointed, because they will die. That's just common sense, right? So something good done at the right time is not a good idea. It's the same with things in your life. Sometimes you may feel that something is the "right thing" but you have to take timing into consideration, or as good as it is, it may just not be right just now.

I am also a firm believer in doing things for the right reason. Doing the right thing for the wrong reason is the wrong thing. Let's use the example of gifts here. I love gifts! I love getting gifts, but I think I love giving them even more. Giving gifts is a good thing, right? Well, that depends. A true gift is something that's given just because. There should be no ulterior motives. There should be no strings attached. So, if you give a gift for any other reason that just that you have a heart full of love and want to bless someone else, you are actually corrupting something very beautiful. This happens a lot. Our motives are not always pure. Others motives are not always pure. Sometimes we do good things with the wrong motivation, and it spoils the good thing.

So what does this have to do with answering the question about whether or not you are limiting yourself and others by setting boundaries? I guess it really all comes down to honesty. There are not too many things more destructive and restrictive than deception. That's why it is so important for you to consider timing, motivation and even just whether or not you even want to say "yes" to something. In their book "Boundaries, When to Say Yes, How to Say No to Take Control of Your Life", authors Cloud and Townsend say it profoundly,

"In other words, if we say yes to God or anyone else when we really mean no, we move into a position of compliance. And that is the same as lying. Our lips say yes but our hearts (and often our half-hearted actions) say no."

Wow! You mean all this time that I thought I was being a good person and taking on things sacrificially when I didn't want to I was being dishonest? Yikes! I have always prided myself in being a very honest person, but this statement proves otherwise. So, saying "no" to the things you don't want to do or are not supposed to do actually makes room for the things you want to do and the things you are supposed to do? That doesn't really seem limiting or restrictive at all now, does it?

Here's another twist. What if by saying no to the things that are not what you want to do or are supposed to do, you know, all the things you are doing out of obligation and because there's "no one else to do it." What if that actually makes space and gives an opportunity to someone else, the person that actually IS supposed to do it? What a concept! You are creating more opportunities for yourself AND for other people, by saying NO! Who knew!

So, are fences limiting to you and to others? It depends on how you look at it. Fences do limit you from being where you shouldn't be and limits others from being where they shouldn't be, which is in each other's yards without permission! It may seem limiting to you if your neighbor isn't taking care of his yard the way he should, but it would be quite awkward and inappropriate for you to march onto her property and re-landscape her yard. Thus, the fence. It provides clarity, and that's a good thing.

The Gift

The first gift, and one that is anything but limiting is that you have the opportunity to clear out the old and make room for the new. In your yard, and in your life. You only have so much time, energy, and resources. Why not spend time on the stuff you were meant to spend time on and fulfill your true purpose on this planet? What could be a greater gift than that?

The second gift you give is getting out of the way so that others have the opportunity to be fulfilled in their own lives. There's nothing more empowering than taking a leap of faith, or taking on a new project, or having the motivation to do something within your gifts to serve the world. If you get out of the way and stop trying to fill in every gap, hopefully that person that needs a job, a project, a purpose will see that there is a need for what they have to offer, and that there is room for them to step forth and expand themselves. Do you see how this is a win-win for everybody? You get to stop doing all the things you didn't want to do and don't even feel like you're good at so that someone else can do what they love and feel like they have something to offer.

Are Fences Causing Me to Be Angry?

Will you experience angry feelings when you begin to set boundaries? Probably. A lot of people do. There's a couple of things that happen when you start on this journey of learning to set limits in your life.

The first thing that happens is that as you begin to read and talk about and notice how other people interact with you, you will become aware of several things:

1) That you don't have any boundaries.
2) That other people disregard any boundaries that you have.
3) That you do not do well when others set boundaries with you.

This can bring up angry feelings for different reasons:

-If you realize that you just don't have any boundaries, you may be angry with yourself for allowing others to walk all over you.

-If you realize that when you have/do try to set boundaries that you are disregarded by others, you may be angry at those people for not respecting you.

-If you realize that you don't do well when others set boundaries with you, you may be angry at yourself because you believe that you are a "bad person", or you may be angry at them because it causes you discomfort that they don't give you what you want.

The interesting thing about any of these angry feelings are that they are not being CAUSED by you being aware of or setting boundaries. That's because nothing has changed. These patterns have probably been happening for a long time, possibly even your whole life. The only thing that has changed is your awareness of what's going on. This may be very uncomfortable. Especially if you tend to be like a lot of people who were brought up that anger is unacceptable or wrong. Just realize that this is normal, and that you can work through it. You are not destined to be an angry, bitter person unless you choose to get stuck there.

The anger that you are experiencing is not happening all of a sudden. It's actually been there for a long time. You just have learned to suppress it or ignore it. It may not feel good at all, but know that it actually serves a purpose. That's right. Anger can actually be your friend. Instead of viewing anger as a bad thing that needs to be done away with, think of it instead as a catalyst to motivate you to get to where you want to be in your life.

So, do fences cause you to be angry? Not only can a fence not make you angry (because it's not a living thing), but neither can another person. Sure, you may be triggered and feel the emotion of anger because of something someone does or says, but you stewing about things is your choice.

Are you angry that you failed to put up a fence and the neighbor's dog keeps pooping in your yard?

Are you angry that your neighbor put up a fence to protect its property, and he blocked your view?

Are you angry that you built a fence and your neighbor just comes through the gate anyway whenever he wants?

Those are legitimate arguments. But you should also be able to see that your anger is under your control. You can put a fence up; dog problem solved. You can talk to your neighbor about the height of the fence, or you can just get over it, it's up to you. You can put a lock on your gate so that you are the only one who has access to your yard. It's your choice.

The Gift

So, what is the gift you receive from anger? It sounds weird to even say it because anger is usually viewed as so damaging and negative.

Anger serves an important purpose. 1) It's a warning signal; telling you that something needs to change. 2) It's a motivator that gives you the courage to do what you need to do.

Sometimes you just need enough motivation to take a step, make a change, put a stop to something, and anger may just be the ticket! You should actually embrace this anger in order to catapult you to a different place. Don't worry. It's not here to stay. It's just here to protect you and let you know that something is not right. You or your boundaries are being violated and it's not okay! It's a reminder that things need to change, and you have the power to change them. In this way, anger becomes a gift.

Once you begin to understand and implement boundaries into your life, you will notice that the anger will actually diminish. So, building fences actually does the opposite of causing anger, they help make it not necessary! What do you think about this phrase: "Don't get mad, get even?" Pretty vindictive, wouldn't you say? I've never thought that was a good principle to live by. Hostility is rarely if ever solved by more hostility. But what about this, "Don't get mad, set a boundary." Ah... Now that might work! And it does! Good news!

> **PROACTIVITY.**
> YOU HAVE HEARD THE PHRASE "DON'T GET MAD, GET EVEN."
> TRY THIS: "DON'T GET MAD, **SET A BOUNDARY.**"

Making Peace with Building Fences

There is no way to address every possible fear and hesitation that people have about setting boundaries. But I'm hoping that we addressed at least some of the more common ones, and that you are starting to understand that in spite of the fear of what could go wrong, there are far more benefits than risks in setting limits. It's the only way to set ourselves up for success in our lives and health in our relationships.

Do the exercises in the workbook that are designed to help you make peace with setting boundaries. Give yourself grace and realize that you are making some huge shifts. It takes time. You will need to process through some of the fear and confusion, but it will become easier and more clear as you embrace this new path. I promise it will be worth it!

Chapter 8

Self-Care

Self-care is not selfish. You cannot serve from an empty vessel.
-Eleanor Brownn

Self-care or self-love has become quite a popular topic these days. I'm glad it has, because it's something that we have not been taught to do very well. A lot of people in my generation, and the generations before me, got the idea that worrying about yourself in any way automatically meant you were selfish. In fact, to think about or do things out of self-interest or concern was considered unspiritual for a lot of people. For some reason, I and many others came to the conclusion that in order to be spiritual and serve others, it had to look like martyrdom and total self-sacrifice. Whether this is a generational thing, or a misinterpretation of Biblical truths, it became engrained for a lot of people, and they accepted it as right and true.

It's so important to remember that building emotional fences is so much more than just a way to protect yourself. Yes, it is about keeping things out of your "yard" that are harmful, but there's a whole other piece that you sometimes forget. Building fences in your life is also about making sure you invite good stuff and good people in. It's not about isolating and cutting yourself off from the rest of the world. It's about deciding what you want your yard (your life) to look like, and opening the gate to things that will help get you there. Self-care is one of those things. You need to let in the good, and once you have, you need to be intentional about taking care of it. Remember, you want to build fences, not walls!

I'm so glad that as I have been on this path of personal development and enlightenment the past 15 years that I have come to realize that self-care is not only far from selfish, it is actually the greatest gift I can give to myself AND to those around me. The same goes for you. Perhaps you have never thought of self-care as a gift to those in your life who you are in relationship with. Let's explore some things that will help you to see what I'm talking about.

It's Necessary

Many view self-care as a luxury, when in fact it really is a necessity. If you are going to operate at your optimum capacity, it is vital for you to take care of yourself--body, mind and spirit. This is not an extra, or something reserved for those who have "earned it." It is necessary to keep you functioning, healthy, and having a positive outlook on life.

I view this in the same way as a lot of the things you do to keep yourself healthy, comfortable, and in good social standing with others. Let's take showering and brushing your teeth, for example. If you don't do it, will it kill you right away? Not likely, but it will make things very uncomfortable. Will it will begin to affect your health and your relationships with others? Definitely.

If you don't brush your teeth, you probably won't see drastic consequences immediately, but it won't take long before you will notice the effects of neglecting this important hygiene practice. It starts out as annoyances like dirty teeth and bad breath, but before long it can lead to social issues such as people not wanting to associate with you because of poor hygiene. Ultimately, it turns into a serious issue leading to decay, tooth loss, and serious health risks that can actually be life-threatening.

If you define necessary as "things I cannot survive without," showering, brushing your teeth, or self-care may not seem to fall into that category. However, it is pretty apparent that without them, life will become difficult and eventually it will affect your health, physically and emotionally.

It's Efficient

If a person can get past viewing self-care as selfish, it doesn't take long to realize that it actually makes a lot of sense. Think about this: If you burn out, or become ill, or die, how much do you think you will be able to do for others? You can think all day long, "Oh, that's so dramatic, and it won't happen to me." Really? How do you know?

It happens to people just like you all the time:

They have nervous breakdowns. So could you.

They come down with debilitating illnesses (which almost always are a product of stress). So could you.

They develop emotional issues due to lack of sleep, depression, effect on relationships. So could you.

They die, and not just of old age. So could you.

This is the reality of the frailty of human life. Our bodies are amazing. We are extremely resilient. But we have our limits.

It's so easy to think:

"Well, I don't have a choice."
"I don't have time to take a break."
"I can't say no, because no one else will do it."

You may believe that's true. Here's the thing, if something happens to you tomorrow, whether simply debilitating or totally tragic, the world will go on, without you.

I'm not saying that you aren't amazing, and important and that your life doesn't matter, but if you can't do "it", whatever "it" is, it will get figured out. Don't wait to self-care until your choices are taken away. Don't run yourself into the ground sacrificing yourself so that the people who love you won't get to have you around. Don't become simply an actor in someone else's play and lose who you are and your ability to give your amazing gifts to the world.

I'm talking about this because I know the price I have paid for not listening to my body, for not taking care of myself emotionally and for sacrificing myself to the point of not feeling like I had anything to offer outside of what I could DO for others. I stuffed, stressed, and strived until my body and my emotional self couldn't suppress any more, and it manifested as a chronic autoimmune illness for me. IT'S NOT WORTH IT!

It's Good Stewardship

"What is stewardship?" and "What does that have to do with self-care?" Stewardship is the careful and responsible management of something entrusted to one's care. You are to be a good steward of everything that has been given to you. What is more precious and sacred than the mind, body, soul, and life that has been so graciously given to you by your Creator?

Are you familiar with the Parable of the Talents in Matthew 25:14-30? It is an interesting and sobering illustration of how you are to handle the gifts you have been given. It can apply to the stewardship of yourself as well. Here's my paraphrase:

A master went on a journey and entrusted his money to his servants. He gave five "talents" to one, two to another, and one to another. The servant with the five talents invested them and doubled his master's money. The servant with two talents invested them and doubled his master's money. The servant with the one talent dug a hole and buried it in the ground, and it did nothing.

When the master returned, he was very pleased with how the first two servants had handled what he had entrusted to them, and he entrusted them with much more because they had proven themselves to be good stewards. However, the master was very unhappy with the servant who had simply buried the money in a hole. His response was, "The least you could have done was put it in the bank where it would have received interest." He took what he had given that servant and gave it to the one who now had ten talents and he fired the servant."

What does this have to do with self-care? You should take great care of this amazing gift that you have been given called life. But you must go above and beyond in cherishing and nurturing it so that you can live up to your full potential so you can do what you were put on this planet to do.

If you are hiding, playing small, not caring and nurturing yourself, you will not be able to fulfill your purpose in the lives of those around you and in the world. God expects each one of us to do our part. It is part of our gratitude to show Him and the world that we do not take for granted what we have been given and that we are fiercely committed to taking care of it to the best of our ability so that we are ready to receive even more.

Have you ever wondered if the reason you do not have the life you want and you have not been blessed with more is because you are not being a good steward of what you have? Take care of the precious gift of you. It's the only way to have the ability to give and love and serve in the highest and most impactful way.

It's Your Job

Unless you are a child who does not have the maturity or capacity to self-regulate and do what is necessary to keep yourself healthy, it is your job, and your job alone to make sure that you take care of yourself.

Remember your "yard" is for you to take care of? Taking care of each area of your yard-life is part of self-care. It's no one else's job to make sure you are doing all the things you need to do in every aspect of your life in order to be healthy and functioning.

If you are unhealthy, stressed out, burned out, exhausted, resentful, sick, bitter, doing too much, taking on the responsibilities of others, etc., YOU are the only one who can change it, and you need to. Stop blaming others for not stepping up. Stop being angry that people are piling things on you. Stop hiding and not using your voice and then being depressed because no one cares how you feel. Do something different.

What Does Self-Care Look Like?

Here are some ways to actually implement self-care into your life and begin the practice of good stewardship.

Being vs. Doing

Our culture in the United States is very focused and often obsessed with doing. It is very easy to equate your value and what you contribute to what you DO. Don't get me wrong. There are things that need to be done. Sometimes you are the one who is responsible to DO them. Doing is important, but it is not everything.

Many other cultures value very different things than we do in the U.S. There have been studies done on areas of the world where people live the longest, and also the healthiest and most fulfilling lives. One of them is documented in the book "The Blue Zones" by Dan Buettner. (This is a great read, by the way, and I would highly recommend it!) In these places, hard work is definitely expected and done. However, the emphasis on times of reflection and social interaction are equally respected. While being productive and having a strong work ethic is important, times of quiet, rest and connection with loved ones is just as important or more so to your health and emotional well-being.

Count the cost of your giving

Not too many people are great at managing their finances. Sometimes they just do things because they seem fairly reasonable, and they can justify them. Sound familiar? I think that reasoning is the same for many people. Here are some examples:

It seems like a good idea.

Buying girl scout cookies (it's for a good cause, and besides they are just yummy).

Taking a friend to lunch (it's kind, it's connection, and they needed to be cheered up).

Helping out someone in need (they are worse off than me. (I'm sure I can find the money somewhere...)

I want to feel good.

Picking up the tab for everyone (I love to give and it makes me feel good to do things for others, so it's worth it if I have to eat macaroni and cheese next week!)

Someone asks me to coffee and I can't afford it (it's embarrassing to say I can't, so I'd rather just do it and figure it out where to squeeze it out of my budget later/robbing Peter to pay Paul syndrome).

I don't want to miss an opportunity.

Investing-in this case I'm talking about using money that is budgeted for something else and putting it into something I "hope" will pay off, but I have no guarantee of that (if I don't do it, I will wonder if I missed the "chance of a lifetime"/ the "golden ticket").

Feeling responsible (How will I feel if I don't help and I find out it caused someone pain or suffering?)

It's just money.

Money is made and spent. (I'll figure it out).

I can recover. (We can just take it out of the food budget).

I don't want to be stingy. (People are more important than money.)

Sometimes we justify things by telling ourselves it's noble, even if it's not a good choice or necessarily our place to step in and help.

All of these scenarios seem fairly benign. None of them are earth-shattering. Several small decisions made with poor judgement can quickly spiral out of control and turn into huge issues for you.

These things seem insignificant until you can't make rent. They don't seem like a big deal until you have to get a title loan on your car to pay bills and then you can't pay the loan and the car goes away, which means so does the job if you can't get to work.

It seems manageable until you realize you can't pay the heating bill in the middle of winter.

It's the same way with setting boundaries. There is a time to give and a time to pull back. Sometimes it's your time to help others, and sometimes you need to take care of yourself, and here is why: You think you can do it and it will all work out. You should be able to sacrifice to help someone out because it's helpful and it makes you feel better about yourself. You give and you give and you give. You ignore your own needs and what your weary body, mind and soul are trying so desperately to tell you. Then one day, it just doesn't work anymore. I can do just about anything for a while. I can go without adequate sleep. I can skip meals or eat bad food. I can work long hours and never rejuvenate. I can pour into the lives of others and deplete yourself. I can do that.... for a while.... until I can't. You can do it also, until one day:

You realize how resentful you are that others are taking from you and you aren't receiving anything in return.

You find that your emotional piggy bank is absolutely empty.

You discover that you are utterly frustrated, exhausted, and physically ill.

You become aware that you are invisible; reduced to playing roles in the lives of those around you, and you don't know who you are any more.

You have allowed this to happen; allowed others to treat you as they do and expect you to help, fix, take care of, clean it up, and that you are the only one who can change that.

The good news is that you can. You can count the cost, and you can decide if it's worth it to keep doing the things you are doing.

Trust Yourself

How do you know when and how to self-care? Well, your body and your spirit know. Sometimes you just have to stop, get quiet, and ask what it is that you need. Get out of your head and tap into your heart. Your heart will tell you what it needs.

RENEWAL.
IT'S TIME FOR YOU TO DO SOMETHING
THAT FEEDS YOUR SOUL AND REPLENISHES YOUR SPIRIT. TAKE THE TIME TO SELF-CARE.

The what, when, and how of self-care is very individual. Give yourself a lot more grace and permission to do what you need to do. Shut out the voices in your head that say:

"You just had a full night's rest, you shouldn't be tired."
"You really need to be doing something more productive."
"How is what you're doing helping you to get to your goal?"

Do these sound familiar?

Yes, things have to get done. Some things will only be accomplished if you do them. Life is not just about pleasure and relaxing. It's not just about striving and trying and burning out. That's not valuable either. So there must be both doing and being. Both working and resting.

How can you know that what you are doing is actually replenishing and nurturing your body, mind, and spirit? There are several ways. Here are some questions you can ask yourself to know if what you consider to be self-care actually is serving its purpose:

-Is what I am doing causing me to feel expansive? In other words, do I feel that I am in touch with the essence of the true me when I engage in this activity? Do I feel like it is helping me to become the person I wish to be?

-When I am engaged in my self-care activity, do I feel the freedom to be exactly who I am and be exactly where I'm at in that moment?

-Does this activity cause me to feel introspective and at peace with myself and the world around me?

-When I engage in self-care in this way, do I notice that I feel safe to be introspective and contemplative about how things are going in my life?

-When I'm in this space, do I feel like I can just notice my feelings and sit with them instead of judging them and trying to talk myself out of them?

-When I am engaged in this form of self-care, do I sense that I can release expectation, stress, and being attached to certain outcomes?

Ways to Self-Care

Rest. Take a nap or at least lie down and sit quietly with your eyes closed and take some deep breaths. Studies have proven that this can make a greater difference than you can even realize.

Spend time with family and friends. It's important to have connections outside of the interaction you have with those your work with.

Take a break. Studies show that you are much more productive for the day when you take at least two 30 minute breaks during the day. Read a book, take a walk, or listen to music.

Take a vacation. Even if you can't afford a full-blown, all-inclusive trip to somewhere tropical, go on a road trip and stay with a friend, do a stay-cation at a local hotel during the week when rates are cheaper, or go camping. Just breaking the routine will do wonders for you. Even a day trip will do wonders for your mindset and your soul.

Practice meditation. There are so many benefits to this simple and totally free practice. All you need is time and a quiet space. If you have never done it before, do some research. It not only will help you feel more connected and at peace, it has major health benefits as well.

Find or create a support group of people. Look for groups who are dealing with the same issues as you or those who want to grow in personal development. Meet-up groups are a great way to connect with people who have similar interests. (Meetup.com)

Find a life coach or therapist. Depending on the issues and stress level you have, it may benefit you to have someone objective to help you work through some things. Chances are that you won't be able to process through big stuff on your own, and even if you can, you will get results much faster if you have someone giving you the tools you need for your situation.

Take time off from a project or person that is draining your energy. You don't have to make a permanent decision right now. Just take a sabbatical from it. Professors do it. Pastors do it. They understand that rejuvenating and getting a fresh perspective is the only way to stay centered and keep from burning out.

Ask for help. That's right, you don't always have to do it all. Be humble and admit that you need or want a hand. Not only will it bring you joy to feel connected and collaborative, you may just bless someone else who is looking for an opportunity to use their own gifts and skills to make a difference. It's a win-win!

Reconnect with nature. There is just something therapeutic, refreshing, revitalizing about doing something outside, in the beauty of Creation, away from the business of the grind that can do wonders for the soul. Take a hike. Go fishing. Paddle a kayak. Go for a bike ride. Walk by the river. You may be amazed at how refreshed and inspired you feel when you do this.

Allow. That may seem like an odd thing to add here, but I am finding that sometimes it's just the only way to unhook and have peace. Sometimes it feels like no matter what I do or how hard I try, nothing works. Ever have days like that? Well, I figure we have two choices; try harder, or let go and let God do something. This is not a cop-out. Sometimes it's just necessary to stop and allow. Maybe what you are dealing with is a test and you need to persevere, but you need to find another way. Allow. Maybe what you are dealing with is a sign that the season is over or this is no longer your path. Allow. Take time to ground yourself, connect with your heart, and make space for whatever needs to happen. It's called clearing--releasing what no longer serves you and making space for something new; perhaps even something better.

Be intentional with your energy. Everybody has a certain amount of energy. Some have a lot more than others. Know yourself. If being around people takes your energy, be intentional about who you spend time with. If you know you have to do something that will leave you spent, make sure you adjust for that and schedule time for renewal. Don't spend energy on things you can't control. Use your energy to create the most value and to make an impact where you can. It is a precious commodity. Don't waste it on people and activities that you can't help.

> **HELPING.**
> HELP SOMEONE WHO IS TRYING TO GET BETTER AND WANTS TO BE HELD ACCOUNTABLE. ANYONE WHO DOESN'T DO THIS DOESN'T WANT HELP.

Saying Yes to Self-Care

I hope this chapter has helped you to reframe some of your thoughts and beliefs about self-care. I pray that you will begin to accept the fact that it needs to be at the core of your well-being regimen. It is not an elective. The sooner you begin to understand this and implement good self-care practices into your life, the sooner you will see the value of it. Saying yes to yourself is the only way you will be able to continue to say yes to those around you.

Remember, it's necessary. It's efficient. It's your job. It's good stewardship. I'd say those are pretty good reasons to take it seriously. Now please, go love yourself. It's worth it.

Chapter 9

Battles

If you listen to your fears, you will die never knowing what a great person you might have been. – Robert H. Schuller

The Fear of Change vs. The Pain of Being Stuck

Here's the truth about human nature: Until the pain of being stuck becomes greater than the fear of changing, we humans will stay stuck. It's true for me. It's true for you. It's true for everyone. If you're analytical about it, you know you don't want to stay where you are. You know you are tired of doing the same things and never getting anywhere. You are tired of all of the unrealized potential, the unknown bliss, and the unfulfilling life and relationships you have created. You stay in that place for far too long, and then you get resentful, either towards yourself or others that you perceive have contributed to your miserable state of being. Why do you stay in that frustrating place for so long? There are several reasons.

The most obvious reason is *fear*. Ugh! Fear! It's so debilitating. It sucks the life out of you. It can cloud the most inspiring vision and the most beautiful dream. You allow it to consume you, to the point of it being the driving motivator for every decision you make. Worst of all, it snuffs out love. There's a scripture that resonates with me, because I have found it to be so true in my life and in the lives of others. It says, "Perfect love casts out fear." Isn't that awesome? As powerful and foreboding as fear seems, there is something that is more powerful, LOVE! I once heard a sermon on this scripture that has stayed with me, and it makes so much sense. The message was that Love and Fear cannot coexist in the same space. Now, that can be bad news if you choose to be governed by fear, because there won't be room for love.

But the opposite is true as well. If you choose to operate from and be motivated by love, fear will just have to find somewhere else to reside!

> **MOTIVATION.**
> **LET EVERYTHING YOU DO COME FROM LOVE.**
> **LOVE INSPIRES.**
> **FEAR DOES NOT.**
> **CHOOSE LOVE.**

Another reason you don't make the changes you need to make is that you are comfortable where you are. Things may be miserable, but somehow you can find comfort in the fact that you know what to expect, and we all do it. Sad, but true.

If you have ever had children, you can probably remember how much they didn't like having their diaper changed. As a parent, you knew it was necessary, healthy, and that ultimately it would be much more comfortable in the long run, but your baby didn't know that! All they knew is that they didn't want to be messed with. They didn't like being exposed. They didn't want to be bothered with the interruption of being changed. But it needed to happen.

The alternative? It would get stinky for them and for others. It weighted them down. It eventually caused discomfort, a rash, and even pain. Yet, they didn't like it. This may seem like a ridiculous example, but is it? How often do we refuse to stop, change what we're doing, clean things up, get rid of the "crap" in our lives and move on to something better for us and also for those around us?

I want to challenge you. The next time you realize that you need to make a change and you are resistant; ask yourself, "How long do I want to wear this poopy diaper?" I know! It's gross! But think about it. It may be warm. It may keep you protected. It may be familiar. It may be yours. But do you really want to stay there?

It Gets Worse Before It Gets Better

While setting boundaries and making changes is necessary and ultimately what will provide for the healthy and fulfilling lives that we all want, it is by no means a path I would call easy.

It is human nature not to make changes until you are in so much pain you just can't stand it anymore. This is why you have operated the way you have for so long. It has worked for you at some level. This makes it hard for you to do what needs to be done. You continue behaviors, whether they serve you well or not, because there has been some sort of payoff.

Jessie knows that McDonald's is not really a healthy choice. She is struggling with her weight, and the doctor has made it clear that this will cause her health issues if she doesn't choose to address it. She even knows that she doesn't really feel that great after she eats because of all of the fat and carbs in that combo meal. She also feels guilty knowing that she could make a better, healthier choice. However, those fries taste so good! The food comes fast, and Jessie instantly feels gratified and comforted as soon as that food hits her mouth. She didn't have to prepare it, and the best part is that it's fairly cheap, and there's no clean-up! Those are definitely pay-offs!

It may even be worth it to Jessie to continue driving through on a regular basis, because there is definitely convenience and enjoyment involved, and she can justify it because she's very busy! It probably won't be until she can't fit into her favorite pair of designer jeans or her doctor informs her that she is pre-diabetic and needs to go on medication that she will find that the cost of her choices causes more pain than changing how she is doing things.

Realize that it's going to be hard for you at first to remember why you started down this new path of setting boundaries and taking control of your life. It may get ugly. Even in the best case scenarios, there is probably going to be a period of tension, stress, and perhaps even great resistance. It is par for the course.

Knowing there could be a period of resistance may help you to have some compassion for the people that you are setting boundaries with. This is going to be a big shock for them. It's going to be unsettling and frustrating. It's going to cause them to be angry, hurt, and frustrated. Be aware of this and be compassionate. Don't decide it's not worth it, because you know it is. You know that something has to change. Change--whether good or bad--is always stressful and disruptive. This is because you are changing the rules and throwing a wrench in the system.

Have you ever worked for a company that decided to make a huge change in their top management? They decided to clean house and bring in a whole new crew of upper management because something was not working and they knew they had to do something drastic?

Joe worked for a company that decided to make a huge change in their top management. His company decided to "clean house" and bring in a whole new crew of upper management because something was not working and they knew they had to do something drastic.

This was a major adjustment for Joe, and frankly, he just didn't appreciate it. He thought things were going along fine. He had no idea that there was a problem with the way things were being done. It was actually quite a shock to him to find out the company felt the need to totally rethink everything.

He found it very stressful to lose people and policies that were familiar to him, especially when he thought things were just fine. Joe's new supervisor was very different from his previous one that he got along so well with. Now, all of a sudden, what he was doing and how he was doing it began to be questioned and new ways of doing things started to be implemented and required. The level of accountability also got bumped up and he started having to answer to people about things that were never inquired about before. This was all very disruptive and frustrating for Joe, and he wondered if it was all really necessary.

This is probably similar to what the people you are setting boundaries with are going to feel like. Things have been working for them. "We've always done it this way, and it's been fine," may be what they're thinking. They may not understand that it actually hasn't been working for you, because you have probably never told them. Give grace. Be compassionate. But don't let it stop you from doing what you need to do. Remember, if you keep doing something that's not working, you can't expect it to ever be different.

This isn't going to be simple or comfortable by any means. You know what you need to do. It's normal to have resistance, to feel guilty, and you're going to have to till the soil before you will be ready to plant the seeds. It can be a painful process.

In times like this it helps me to remember that the right thing is rarely the easy thing, but in the end, it is still the thing that needs to happen.

Battles with Others

Let's face it, most people do not love conflict. Some of us go to great lengths to avoid it, and I understand, because I am one of those people. This is one of the biggest reasons people decide it's just not worth it to shake things up by changing the rules and setting boundaries with those in their lives. Chances are, there will be moderate to severe resistance. This can't be avoided, but it helps to understand some of the things that may happen and also comforting to know that it's pretty typical.

Addressing The Fear

The biggest obstacle we have when we consider setting boundaries and taking our power back is fear. Although fear is not inspiring nor a healthy motivation for making decisions or choosing your life's direction, it can have a pretty big voice and can keep you from doing the things you need to do in order to create a healthy and successful life. Let's talk about some of the fears that hold you back from setting and enforcing healthy limits with those you are in relationship with. This will be useful as you continue to process what it will actually look like when you begin to implement boundary principles.

What's True

When you begin to change the rules and set new boundaries and start speaking the truth about what you want and need in your life, there are many possibilities, and many of them may trigger fear in you.

Others may feel abandoned by you. Chances are that you have had trouble setting boundaries in the past because you are a caring, giving, nurturing and compassionate person. When you begin to be more selective and caring about your giving, it may be hard for others, and they may take it personal. Depending on how much they count on you to care for them and nurture them, they may feel emotionally deserted and even hurt to some extent.

Others may disapprove of you or feel disappointed by you. You may have people that because of their own misconception or distorted thinking assume that you have suddenly turned into a self-serving and uncaring person. Realize this is their perception, either because you have always been compliant and it works well for them, or because they themselves do not have a healthy grasp on setting or respecting the limits of others.

Others may get angry with you. Remember that anger is a form of control. Some people have used anger to get what they want, and it has worked well for them, perhaps even in their relationship with you. When you don't just cave in to what they want, they are going to try to ante' things up to see if they can still control you. Anger is also something that people project, so it may not be as much about you as it is about anger with themselves or someone else. It can also be that they are frustrated because they have never learned to get what they need in a healthy way.

Others (and you) may feel discomfort in the relationship. This is especially true if you have been operating in a certain way and been in the relationship for a long time. When you begin to speak up and not tolerate things that you have always seemingly been okay with, it will change the dynamics of the relationship, and it will probably feel quite awkward.

You may experience increased conflict. On top of things being uncomfortable and awkward, you may experience some conflict in varying degrees. Whether the other person is doing it intentionally or not, they may apply some pressure, especially if they know that you usually do anything to avoid conflict. Approach this as a "test" of some sort, and know that even though it is really unpleasant, and albeit upsetting, if you hold your ground, chances are it will diminish over time or even subside.

Others may judge you. You may find, especially with manipulative and controlling people that you receive judgement from them. People judge in lots of ways, and if you care about what people think, it can be painful and cause you to question your new way of doing things. Judgement may show up as character assessment, misinterpreting your motives and intentions, and sometimes even spiritual abuse which we addressed in Chapter 5. **Who you are; your integrity, your character, your heart, your principles, those are things that don't change unless you make a decision to change them.** What someone else thinks about you does not change who you are. You are who you are, and you do not have to prove or justify that to anyone. Your actions are a product of who you are; but someone's bias, judgement, or filter cannot ever change who you are. Trust yourself regardless of the opinions and assumptions of others, no matter who they are, and how much you care about them.

Swallowed Up

You may be fearful when you begin the journey of setting boundaries that other people's reactions are out of your control. It's okay because you are not responsible for them anyway. Feelings, reactions, and behaviors are all the responsibility of the person who owns them. Period.

You've probably heard the saying, "Feel the fear, and do it anyway." That is so appropriate when it comes to boundary-setting. You may experience some things that feel like you can't push through. You may feel fearful, hurt, uncomfortable, unsure, selfish, or guilty. It's okay. Feel your feelings. Sit with them for a while, but don't allow them to take over. Acknowledge the fear; just don't let it stop you from doing what you know you need to do.

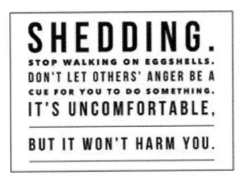

Dealing with Reactions of Others

You cannot control the reactions of others. Truth be told, you cannot even make someone honor the boundaries you have set. However, there are some tools that I use in my own life and in my coaching that I think help a lot.

Neutral energy. You can set boundaries and have hard conversations without being defensive, angry, or controlling. The way to do that has very little to do with what you say, and mostly to do with the energetic space you come from. We all know that the words we use are not nearly as powerful as the body language we have and the tone with which we say what we say. I'm not saying that there is no such thing as harsh language, verbal abuse, or inappropriate conversation. For the most part, the delivery of the content generally has the most power. Boundaries should be set not with the intention of demanding, mandating, or punishing, but with the intention of making clear what we will or will not do. Because of this, you can set a boundary with kind words, coming from a grounded space and a confident yet neutral energy.

> **TEMPERANCE.**
> **BE KIND; GENTLE.**
>
> **DON'T ALLOW THE WAY YOU FEEL TO BE AN EXCUSE TO TREAT OTHERS CARELESSLY.**

Good support. It's important to have relationships in place that are healthy. You need feedback and encouragement from people who can be more objective about why you need to change the way you are doing things in your life. If you do not have anyone like that in your life, you make it a priority to start building connections with other people who are heading the same direction as you are in life. Find a support group. Take personal development classes. Get coaching. Go to therapy. Spend time with people that leave you better than they found you instead of ones who drain your energy and leave you feeling more empty and frustrated. Having support may not seem crucial right now, but I promise it is necessary if you want to be successful on this journey.

Keeping the end goal in mind. Sometimes when you begin to experience the discomfort of the reactions of others, you may find yourself questioning if this was really necessary and even a good idea. When you begin to feel this way, try to remember what you were feeling like when you made the decision to do things a different way. Go back and look at your journal. Ask your friends to remind you how miserable you have been. Remember that what you were doing was not working and you were fed up. You can go back to the old way. It's your choice. But is that what you really want? And why did you start down this path? Is it because you could envision something better for yourself? Is it because you realized that your life was chaotic and unmanageable and you were sick and tired of feeling that way? Try to remember THAT. Now count the cost, and decide if it's worth it.

Stay grounded and consistent. Be compassionate with others. This isn't easy for them either. But in your compassion, do not cave in. You are strong. You are smart. You are capable. And you deserve to be healthy emotionally. The only way for that to happen is for you to tolerate the resistance, the discomfort, and the guilty feelings, and come out on the other side. You will find that you are more responsible, more giving, more loving, and able to live your life without losing yourself and becoming resentful and sick. Set boundaries. Have consequences. Stay with it. It works.

Have mantras that make boundaries clear. Sometimes it helps to just have a few things that you have thought about ahead of time that you can use in different scenarios when you feel caught off guard or unprepared. Maybe you can think of some on your own, but here's a few to start with. (Make sure you tweak them so that they feel authentic and congruent with who you are.)

"That's not going to work for me right now."

"I'm not comfortable with the way you touched me, spoke to me, addressed me..."

"I don't feel that I am the best person for that job, task, position at the present moment."

"I am unable to commit to anything else right now."

"I need some time to think about whether or not that will work for me. Can I get back to you?"

"I love you, or care about you, and I am not able to help you right now."

I think you get the idea, and you can probably add some of your own. It's great to have some comebacks "pre-rehearsed," especially if you are someone who needs time to process or ends up giving in to things you regret later because you don't do well under pressure.

> **CONTEMPLATE.**
> **FEELING PRESSURED TO MAKE A DECISION?**
>
> ASK FOR TIME TO PROCESS. IT'S OKAY NOT TO GIVE AN **ANSWER IN THE MOMENT.**

Don't get caught up in excuses or explanations. I love the phrase, "No is a complete sentence." It may sound harsh, but trust me, if someone is going to be upset about you setting a boundary, they probably are not going to care about why you set it. If you are in a close relationship and you want to give more detail about why something doesn't work for you, that's fine, but start realizing it's okay to decline without going into a big litany of excuses. "No, I can't," should be enough of an answer, and it will be for those who have boundaries of their own.

Remember: You can't control other people's reactions. They will either change, or they will refuse. If they refuse, you either have to let them walk away, or choose to walk away yourself. In this situation, there is a true risk in setting boundaries, but it is also very telling about the relationship. Do what you know you need to do for yourself and even for the good of the other person. Then let go. Take responsibility for what is yours, and let them own what is theirs as well.

Fear vs. Truth

Still having a hard time deciding if the conflict and discomfort are worth it? Maybe it will help you to have a visual. Remember the old "pros and cons" list that you make when you're trying to make an important decision? Sometimes that's just the kind of process that helps you to really take an objective look at what your options are and which is better for you.

Fear: If I set a boundary, the other person may feel abandoned by me.

Truth: If I set a boundary, the other person may have the opportunity to take responsibility for something they are completely capable of, and it will build their self-esteem and self-confidence.

Fear: If I set a boundary, the other person may disapprove of me or be disappointed in me.

Truth: If I set a boundary, it may cause the other person to realize that a relationship is give and take and they may learn how to honor other people's limits and needs.

Fear: If I set a boundary, the other person may get angry with me.

Truth: I cannot control whether or not someone gets angry with me, and I cannot cause someone to be angry with me. If I set a boundary, they may have to find another way to relate and communicate and ultimately learn to compromise.

Fear: If I set a boundary, it may cause discomfort in the relationship.

Truth: If I set a boundary, it's possible that the other person may experience what it feels like to be uncomfortable instead of just me being the one who's uncomfortable all the time.

Fear: If I set a boundary, it will cause conflict in the relationship.

Truth: If I set a boundary, there may be conflict, which could lead to hard conversations, but ultimately a mutual relationship instead of just me walking on eggshells.

Fear: If I set a boundary, the other person may judge me.

Truth: If I set a boundary, I might figure out who really respects me for who I am, and I may figure out that I don't need critical and judgmental people in my life.

Sometimes it is even more helpful to project into the future. What I mean by that is: sometimes it's necessary to ask yourself some hard but crucial questions:

"If everything stays the same as it is right now, what will my life look like in 1 year? 3 years? 5 years?"

"If I change my patterns and start setting boundaries and taking care of myself, what will my life look like in 1 year? 3 years? 5 years?"

"If I continue to ignore what my body is telling me, what will my health be like in 1 year? 3 years? 5 years?"

"If I begin taking care of myself and listening to what my body, mind and spirit need, what will my life look like in 1 year? 3 years? 5 years?"

"If this relationship continues down this path and nothing changes, what will the relationship be like in 1 year? 3 years? 5 years?"

"If I begin to set boundaries and strive for more communication and healthier functioning in my relationship, what will it look like in 1 year? 3 years? 5 years?"

"If I continue in this profession, career, relationship, what will my state of mind, self-esteem and outlook on life be in 1 year? 3 years? 5 years?"

"If I end this profession, career, relationship now, what will my state of mind, self-esteem and outlook on life be in 1 year? 3 years? 5 years?"

None of us has a crystal ball. You can't possibly know exactly what life will be like down the road, but for some of you, you know that the situation you are in or the way you are operating is not sustainable, and probably has no chance of getting better. What are you going to do about it? It's your choice. Stay there as long as you need to. Just know that whenever you are ready, there is another way. It's not easy, but you have everything you need to pursue it...when you're ready.

Battles with People You Can't Help

I am probably one of the most hopeful, optimistic people you will ever meet. I'm not saying that to brag. Sometimes it's a great thing. Sometimes it's not. The times it is not is when I want so desperately to break the other person through or want the relationship to work so badly I push aside the reality of the situation. I'm not going to go into depth about this list of people you can't help, and I would never want to say there's no hope for someone. I believe there is always hope. God does miracles. People break through. Lives get turned around. This only happens with fierce intention, accountability and a lifelong commitment by the person with the issue to stay on track. That being said, here are a few people you can't help.

The Abuser

The Addict

The Narcissist

The Mentally Ill

The Perpetual Victim

In these situations, professional help is necessary. Also, willingness on the part of the person to get well, and stay well is the only way it works. Strict accountability and getting up every day with the intention of remaining sober, healthy, or non-violent is the only way people overcome situations like these.

If you want something more for the other person or for the relationship than what the other person wants, it is not going to happen and it won't work. You can't want it worse for them than they do for themselves.

It's also important to realize people in these situations are not in a healthy space. They are not able to process and react to information the same as someone who is emotionally healthy. Just remember, you can't have a rational conversation with someone who doesn't have the ability to reason. I spent a lot of years not understanding this, and now that I do, it saves me a lot of energy and effort in situations that are way over my head.

Boundaries themselves will not be enough for these people to change what they're doing. You need to protect yourself and let them do their own work, as hard as it is to watch someone destroy their life.

> **ELIMINATE.**
> WHAT ARE YOU "PUTTING UP" WITH?
>
> **AREN'T YOU TIRED OF IT?**
> IT'S TIME TO SAY "NO MORE" AND STOP SUBJECTING YOURSELF TO IT.

Battles with Yourself

Often times you have a battle within yourself that prevents you from doing what you want to do and know you should do. Let's talk about some of these internal battles. Here are some questions that may go through your mind when you are seriously contemplating how to start setting limits with those you are in relationship with.

What if I can't follow through? It's a legitimate concern. Maybe you have had a hard time with consistency and follow through and it makes you doubt whether or not it's possible. I'm here to tell you it is. Start with smaller boundaries that aren't quite so "risky", and being committed to not to backing down. Choose things that will not be too threatening at first so you can build your "boundary-setting muscles."

What if they go off the deep end if I step back? I know what it feels like to wonder if drawing a line will result in someone walking away, taking their life, ending up on the street, etc. I would like to tell you that it won't happen, but the truth is, it might. What I know from my own experiences is that you can't control any of that. You may be able to delay it, but you cannot prevent it. You are simply prolonging the inevitable and living in a state of false hope. If a person doesn't want to stay in a relationship, if they don't want to be alive, if they don't want to do what it takes to be able to function and take care of themselves, you will not be able to stop it. Sometimes setting the boundary is the only hope they have of waking up and realizing that they have to decide to change, and that is the best you can hope for. And sometimes it happens.

What if they are dependent on me physically or financially? First of all, it's important for me to ask "why?" Why are they dependent on you physically? Why are they dependent on you financially? Is it because they truly are not capable of taking care of themselves? There are situations like that, but is this one of them?

Unless a person is a minor child, or a disabled or incapacitated adult, you are not responsible for them physically or financially. Remember when we talked about the difference between being responsible for and responsible to? Yes, you should care, support emotionally, encourage; but you shouldn't have to take care of them if they are able to take care of themselves.

Someone not WANTING to take care of themselves physically or financially is not the same as not being ABLE to. I'm going to go out on a limb here and say that even if you are caring for someone physically or financially because they cannot do it themselves, you can have boundaries. If you are footing the bill. If they live in your house. If you are giving up income and time to help them, there are some reasonable things you should expect from them. Respect, cooperation, contribution--these are just a few.

What if you don't feel worthy of speaking up, saying what you need, or creating the life you want? This is a tough one because no one can convince you that you are worthy. This is a self-esteem issue, and it boils down to your core value. Everyone has intrinsic value--you have worth simply because you exist. It has nothing to do with external things, which means you can't create more worth, and you can't cause it to be less. If you find yourself struggling with intrinsic value and self-esteem, you would do well to work with a coach or therapist to build it up. You need to know that you matter. Everyone deserves to be heard. Everyone deserves to be loved. Everyone deserves to offer their gift to the world.

Chapter 10

Victories

What lies behind us and what lies before us are tiny matters compared to what lies within us. – Henry Stanley Haskins

Someone told me one time, "Feelings are rarely accurate indicators of reality." I tend to agree. Feelings need to be acknowledged and validated, however, they shouldn't be allowed to be in charge.

Even when you are setting boundaries in a healthy and grounded way, it may not feel very good, but don't get discouraged! You will get more comfortable and confident with your fence-building over time.

You are probably familiar with one or more of these quotes:

"No pain, no gain."

"It's hard until it's not."

"Hard work pays off."

"Nothing works until you do."

Even though it may not feel like it, if you are experiencing discomfort, you are making more progress than you think!

How Will You Know You Are Making Progress?

Are you experiencing any of these things?

> *Not as much fulfillment or connection in current relationships.*
>
> *Frustration with others who are resisting and not honoring your limits.*
>
> *Not as tolerant of others' behavior.*
>
> *Spending time or wanting to spend time with healthy people.*

Noticing what you love and honoring it.

More in tune with your body, mind and spirit and aware of the need for self-care.

Taking baby steps. Setting small boundaries in safe places.

Taking big steps. Setting boundaries in significant relationships.

Okay with being uncomfortable with people's reactions.

Spending your energy on what you can control.

Not engaging in the helplessness or drama of others.

Getting your needs met in creative ways instead of being resentful.

Being happy that others are living their lives and making their own choices.

Being happy for the success of others.

Using your voice and letting go of the results.

Trust yourself and the process.

Saying no to legitimate need and not feeling quite so guilty.

Noticing and respecting the choices of others.

Noticing others boundary issues.

Saying no first when you're not sure.

Not giving as many excuses.

Reminders

Sometimes when things get really uncomfortable and you begin to question yourself, it's hard to remember why you decided to go down this road of building fences. This is a great time to talk about what things will look like as you progress on this journey.

Freedom for Everyone

Although the people you set boundaries with may not be excited about it, and you may not be thrilled with the effects of other people setting boundaries with you, it truly is a beautiful thing. It really is the way it is supposed to be, and it's healthy. It doesn't feel good to be told no or to have limits set on you. It doesn't feel good to others when you set limits with them, but that's just because we haven't been good about clarifying what's ours and taking responsibility for it. The good news is that if you stick with it, you will begin to see how building fences makes your life and your relationships work so much better!

I always tell people who take my course, "It will probably get worse before it gets better." While that doesn't seem very encouraging, it's real. This is not an easy path. It takes a lot of courage, consistency and intentionality. But I promise it will be worth it.

Things really are as they should be when everyone is free to choose. Freedom to create the life you want, and you can also give that gift to someone else. Let go of what you want for others. You worry about your life. Let others choose and learn and grow.

Making Room for the New

It's painful to realize that some of your relationships will change when you begin to set boundaries. Even if you know it needs to happen, change is hard. It's even more unsettling to realize that some of the relationships or situations you have been participating in are not in your best interest.

I am one of those Pollyanna, sentimental, hopeless romantics that wants to believe that when I love someone and they love me, that it will be a forever thing. Now as I approach turning 50 years old, I realize that it's just not typical to have jobs, friends, or situations that last a lifetime. If you are the exception, and you still have your best friend from grade school, have been married to the same person for a long time, or live in the same house and have the same career you had when you started your adult life, that's awesome, as long as it's healthy.

A lot of times the people and circumstances that come into our lives are there to teach us something, and the lessons can be all different lengths of time. This is beautiful. It is also hard for those of us who are fiercely loyal or get attached very easily. What has helped me with the pain of losing relationships that have ended or transitioned into something different is that they served their purpose in my life, no matter how long they stayed.

Sometimes you have to really do some introspection and searching and decide if the situations you are in and the relationships you have are actually growing and expanding you into all you are called to be. If they are, great! If they aren't but you can see that they can be improved, awesome! But if they are no longer serving their purpose, and if they are hindering you, and there is little to no hope that they will ever be different, it is time to let go.

Letting go. That's a hard one. Even when you know you need to release something, there is resistance. Pain. Grief. I've never liked goodbyes. I've never thought it felt good to be separated from something or someone that has been a part of my history, as long as it had some value.

Here's some perspective that has helped me: I don't want to minimize the loss. You need to work through it. There will be grief and sadness. But there's another side to this that actually is positive. I call it "clearing"--getting rid of the old which no longer serves you. It's not just about getting rid of the old, it's about making room for the new! And it gets even better! Sometimes you are making room for something even BETTER than you ever thought possible.

> **POSSIBILITIES.**
> SAYING "NO" TO ONE THING GIVES YOU THE FREEDOM TO SAY "YES" TO SOMETHING **ELSE, MAYBE EVEN SOMETHING BETTER.**

Did you ever have to move and change schools as a child? Were you devastated? Did you have to leave people you loved and friends that you were comfortable with? Did you think your heart would break? And then, when you went to the new school, were you terrified? Did you wonder if you would ever be okay and if anyone would even like you or notice you?

I remember this feeling. I was very shy and sensitive as a child, and these kind of situations felt devastating. I remember my first day at a new school and how terrified I was, until that little girl with the ponytails and the blue dress asked me to play on the monkey bars at recess. It was like my world opened up. A new friend! Minutes before I wondered if my little heart would ever stop hurting, and all of a sudden, I had a friend and everything was right again! If I wouldn't have left the old school, I wouldn't have come to my new school and found my new friend!

That's how it feels in life sometimes. You think you will live in the same house, have the same friends, retire from the same job, and then life happens. Either by your choice, or someone else's, everything shifts, and you don't know if you can make it or if you will ever be okay. Then as you begin to adjust to your new situation, you figure out that you weren't even all that happy with where you lived, or who you hung out with or with that job you thought was such a great fit. Sometimes it's even like a weight being lifted off of you. You realize that you hung onto whoever or whatever it was because it was familiar. It was what you had always done. It was what you had always known. But you realize that it wasn't really the best thing for you. And suddenly when you release it, or it releases you, a whole new world opens up. It happens all the time. It's terrifying, and it's beautiful.

More Good News

As you mature in your boundary setting and build your limit-setting muscles, the process will get shorter. You become aware sooner, you set boundaries more promptly, and in turn things resolve into whatever they will be. As you begin to see how effective it is to live and operate this way, it will prompt you to tolerate less pain and not allow as much time to go by before you adjust what is not working. It may be down the road a little way, but eventually it will actually become like second nature to operate in a grounded way.

Coming from a Grounded Space

You will know that you are growing and becoming more proactive when you find yourself moving from being angry and resentful to grounded and capable of taking care of yourself emotionally.

When you start out, unaware of what boundaries mean or how they fit into your life, you are coming from a purely defensive space. You are hiding, or doing what you need to do to avoid conflict because you don't want to be uncomfortable. Unfortunately, this doesn't accomplish what you think it will. You end up feeling frustrated, exhausted, and invisible.

> **BRAVERY.**
> **STOP HIDING.**
> **COME OUT INTO THE LIGHT.**
> **TAKE A STEP AND THEN ANOTHER.**
>
> **YOU WILL KNOW WHAT TO DO WHEN YOU GET THERE.**

When you begin to learn about boundaries, you become aware of the fact that you haven't set any or that others don't respect them even if you do. You feel the resentment and anger begin to creep in. Anger at yourself for teaching people that it's okay to treat you the way they have been, and anger at them because they have been disregarding you and walking all over you for a long time.

Then, as you begin to be more proactive about engaging in healthy relationships and setting new limits on the old ones, you realize that you don't have to be angry anymore. You set the boundary, enforce the consequence, and allow the other person to do what they will. You let the chips fall where they may.

Suddenly you are coming from a confident, grounded space, and it feels really good. You know what you're responsible for. You know what you can and can't control. You want people in your life that are healthy and want to be there. That's who you attract! Suddenly you realize that your life has become fulfilling, doable, and manageable; and you wonder why you didn't figure this out much sooner. It's okay. It doesn't matter. The important thing is that you are doing it now, and it's working!

Eyes Wide Open

Another thing you will notice that will be a confirmation of the victory you are experiencing is that you will notice unhealthy people and drama before they ever get close enough to affect your life! It's like having a "drama" radar! This is definitely the best time to decide if you want this person to come into your yard and into your life.

You will also notice that you are beginning to be drawn to and attracting different people to yourself. Healthy people. Boundary people. People who are responsible for their own lives and who expect you to be responsible for yours.

Relationship Sweet Spots

Remember the "pendulum"? It's true that anytime things go to an extreme, they get out of balance and don't operate the way they should. This is especially true in relationships.

When someone is codependent, they are rescuing, enabling, and perpetuating poor behavior in someone else. This is not good. It may seem helpful, but if you really look at it in the light of truth, responsibility, and emotional health, you will quickly realize it is not a good way to support someone.

When someone is independent, the pendulum swings clear the other way. They are self-sufficient, disconnected, and have trouble giving and receiving. I suppose it depends on your definition of independent whether or not it has a positive or negative connotation. The way I'm using it now is not necessarily the healthiest model for a relationship. We were created to be in relationship. We all operate best with connection and support. There is power in collaboration, and independence in this instance represents disconnection, isolation, and an "each one for himself" philosophy that can be limiting and lonely.

So what's the answer? It's called interdependence--it is where healthy, fulfilling lives, and relationships operate at their highest potential. It's about everyone doing their part. Everyone carrying their load. Everyone being responsible for their property. But all of this without disconnection, isolation, and the feeling of being left to do life completely on your own.

It's about knowing you are cared for and supported. It's about empowering others to do their own work and live their best lives. It's about people being there for each other when life gets too big and unmanageable. It's about everyone reciprocating the give and take so that we all get where we need to go, and we are healthy and whole when we get there. How beautiful is that?

Replacing a Wall with a Fence

You will know you are making progress when you build enough confidence and safety in your life that you are able to take down some of the walls you put up to protect yourself, and you replace them with fences that allow you to be connected while at the same time remaining grounded and preserving individuality.

In some situations, the wall can never come down. You should never subject yourself to abuse and mistreatment, and it is important to do whatever necessary to protect yourself emotionally. However, there will be times where people change. They come around. They get on a new path. As long as they show a significant and consistent pattern of change, it may be possible to restore a relationship with them.

With others, it's just a matter of you getting really clear about what is yours and what is not. What you want for your life, and how to protect that. How to get your needs met and not give to your own detriment. Once you figure that out and have some tools and support, you will begin to live your life and build your relationships on your own terms.

One of the greatest things about boundaries is that they are yours. You can renegotiate them. You can get rid of them when they are no longer necessary. You can tighten them and loosen them as needed depending on the other person or the situation. This is all within your control.

You also can rest assured that this is a process, and it's okay if you aren't an expert at setting limits at first. This is a skill. It takes time to figure out what works, and sometimes you won't do it just right. It's okay if you don't do it perfect! It's not set in stone. Just adjust it and move forward. Remember that doing something imperfectly is better than doing nothing at all, and that includes boundary setting.

Letting Go of Results

You will also know you are growing and maturing on your boundaries journey when you become okay with the reactions of others. You may not necessarily like the response, and it may not be what you were hoping for, but you realize that you can be kind, be compassionate, and still do what you need to do. You are learning to set the boundaries that are necessary for you to keep yourself safe emotionally, and then you are able to let go of the results, knowing that everyone involved is at choice.

Of course, the best-case scenarios are the ones where you make the boundary known, and the other person acknowledges and respects it.

I've had situations like this. One situation was very difficult and quite painful. It involved a close family member that was continuing to verbally abuse and attack me. I finally decided that the only way to get a break from the behavior and hopefully shift the relationship was to take a total break from communicating. It nearly broke my heart, but I realized that things had escalated to the point where it simply couldn't continue the way it was going.

After five months, we decided to reconnect and see how it went. I made it clear that as much as I wanted the relationship to work, I was not willing to have things go back to the way they were before. I am happy to say that the relationship is amazing. There is respect and love and connection as there never was before. The boundary actually provided an opportunity for us both to heal and renegotiate that relationship, and it is now one of the best relationships I have.

Contrast that with what happened when I set a hard boundary with my husband. After years of deception, addiction, and enabling, something broke inside me and I knew I had to draw the line. In my mind, I just needed a couple of days to clear my head and figure out how to move forward in my marriage that had been unhealthy for about 10 years.

I made a decision to go and stay with a friend so that I could make a plan and make a point. I could no longer tolerate the lies and denial, and I needed to say "enough". I sat my kids down (they were in high school at this point) and told them what I was doing and why. I told them they could come with me if they wanted (they were not in danger staying at home with their dad). They declined and I proceeded with what I thought would be a very short and temporary situation.

After a couple of days, the response was not what I anticipated at all. My husband wanted to know why I was overreacting. He wanted to know what my problem was. He wanted to know when I was going to stop being ridiculous and come home. This was not what I expected. I thought that drawing the boundary would compel him to realize that we were in crisis. I hoped he would realize what was at risk and it would prompt him to take the steps needed to save our marriage and our family. But that didn't happen.

As 2 days turned into 4, and then 6 and then 10, things continued to spiral downward. I started to see the true condition of the relationship. Things came to the surface through him and other people offering information, and I could see things clearly that I was oblivious to before, or that I just didn't want to believe were possible. As the days went by, it became obvious that he was not willing to shift or change or attempt to try anything different to save the relationship. I was heartbroken. This was not what I wanted or thought would ever happen.

Worst case scenario: The other person does not respect the boundary, honor it, or have the desire to do what it takes to create a healthy situation or restore the brokenness in the relationship. It is surreal. It is devastating. But it is also truth-telling.

Both of these situations are valuable, although one is definitely preferable over the other. The boundary exposes the true nature of the relationship and the intentions of the other person. It gives the opportunity for healthy dialogue and renegotiation of things that are just not healthy and definitely not working. It also provides the clarity and reality check that is needed when a relationship has no hope and continuing in unhealthy patterns means prolonging the inevitable.

Whatever the outcome, even though it may not feel like it, it is a victory no matter what. It's either the thing that saves the relationship, or helps us to end the relationship in order to make room for new people and things that will support us and help us to expand and grow.

EXPRESS.
USE YOUR VOICE.

YOU HAVE A MESSAGE.
WHAT YOU HAVE TO SAY MATTERS.
SPEAK YOUR TRUTH AND
LET GO OF THE RESULTS.

Chapter 11

A Better Day

Letting go means to come to the realization that some people are a part of your history, but not part of your destiny. – Steve Maraboli

Remember Chapter 2? We talked about all the things that just weren't working, and although it seemed overwhelming you should not to give up. Aren't you glad you stuck with it? I want to encourage you even more by showing you what it looks like when you begin setting boundaries, working on yourself, and following your path.

I can tell you this from experience, and from watching the lives of those who have taken my courses and whom I have coached. It's so fulfilling to see someone who came to me so distraught and frustrated and with no hope move to a place of "Angie, this is working!" If you will continue on this journey and keep working on boundaries and personal development, your life will start working!

This is Working!

Allowing

Trying harder doesn't work! Sometimes no matter how hard you try, you just can't change something or make it work. The great news is it's not your job to make everything work! That should be a relief to you.

A few weeks ago, I had one of "those" weeks. It seemed like everything I attempted, every door I tried to walk through just slammed in my face. I know there's always resistance in life in one area or another, but it literally seemed like the harder I tried, the more I got shut down. I was beyond frustrated. I was ready to sell my belongings and drive away into the sunset.

People that know me well know that I tend to be a very optimistic, positive person. Even when things seem discouraging, I can usually muster up some hope and encouragement for me and those around me. Well, after about 3 days of being in a really bad space emotionally and mentally, I decided I was done with that! I had a little pep talk with myself and said, "Angie, tomorrow is a new day! Change your attitude; muster up some hope and make the rest of this week awesome!"

I went to bed feeling pretty good about my new outlook on life. Early in the morning I was awakened by a text that delivered some less than happy news. Something that had actually gone right during the week and seemed like a prospective success was not going to happen. Seriously?? I wasn't even awake or out of bed yet. So much for mustering up a great attitude and being hopeful about my future.

I was so over it that I couldn't even get angry. I couldn't even cry. I was at a total loss, and I honestly had no idea where to go from there. I did the only thing I felt I could do in that moment. I threw my hands in the air, palms angled up, and I said "I give...." Oh, I wasn't giving up. I knew that wasn't an option. But I knew I had to give in. It was time to surrender.

It was crazy. In that moment, something happened. The only way I know how to explain it is I just released everything. I told God, "I will take advantage of the opportunities that come my way. I will walk through the doors that open. But I'm done striving. I can't do it anymore. It's sucking the life out of me." I went into a new space of Allowing. Oh, I questioned myself. Even though I felt a sense of peace, I felt a little guilty. Was I quitting? Was I walking away from the hard stuff? Wait, that wasn't it at all. I wasn't quitting, I was letting go, and that's a very different thing.

Sometimes when you don't know what to do, and you are at the end of your resources, emotional reserves, answers, ideas, the only thing to do is to let go and allow your path to unfold ahead of you. You don't have to know all the answers, and you won't. You don't have to make everything happen, and you can't. But you can listen to your heart. You can listen to God. You can take the next step without forcing something to happen. You may have barely enough light to see where the next step is. It's okay. It's enough. When you are ready, the next step will be illuminated, and then the next. You know all you need to know for the moment. Be okay with that.

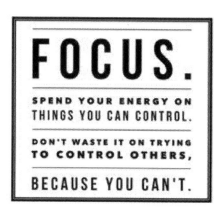

Acknowledging

Minimizing doesn't work! Being in denial about how things really are and downplaying things that need to be dealt with only perpetuates the problem. Acknowledging is not about blaming, nor is it about acting like things are "fine" when they aren't. It's about being aware of the actual condition of things so that you have the ability to deal with them effectively. Be honest about injustice or hurtful behavior. Don't subject yourself to mistreatment, that doesn't do others or you any good at all.

Sometimes you just need to take an honest look at the present state of your life and relationships. This is never easy, especially if you want to look at the bright side all the time. I know it's uncomfortable. I know it's not fun. But it's necessary to get honest with yourself, especially when things are not going very well.

You don't have to change anything right now. Be open to the possibility that things are not working, but that they could be different if you choose to do some things in a different way. Acknowledging and awareness are the first steps to stopping what's not working and becoming aware of what will.

You need to acknowledge your responsibility in what's going on. You can't control everything, but be accountable for the rare cases that you have no contribution in what is happening or the outcome of things. Usually you can find at least a small part that you could have done or can do better or differently. This is not about beating yourself up. There is no point in dwelling on the past and lamenting over it. However, it is always helpful to look back if you are doing it in order to gain information and understand.

When you look honestly at how things went and what you did to contribute, you can see what worked and what didn't. You can try to have compassion toward others who did what they did. This is all very valuable because it is your teacher. It also can take you out of victim mode and help you to forgive and move on with more clarity for the future.

One of the benefits of acknowledging is understanding that you can trust yourself! Dip into your intuition. You will know what to do if you get quiet and listen to your heart.

Next, practice self-love. Acknowledge that sometimes you don't give yourself enough grace and care. It's easy to get caught up in caring and giving to others and neglecting yourself, but you need to remember to love and nurture YOU.

Acknowledge if you are tolerating poor behavior from others. Be honest with yourself if you are dissatisfied with your relationships and your life. Ask yourself why you are settling instead of leaving people and things behind that are holding you back from pursuing your call in life. Think of someone you care about a lot--your spouse, a child, a friend. Would you be okay with them putting up with what you're putting up with? If you say no, then why are you okay with having different standards for yourself? You can't control everything, but you don't have to put up with abusive, manipulative behaviors from others. It's time to put a stop to it. You're worth more than that.

Creating Your Life

Being a martyr doesn't work! Get honest with yourself about this. Take responsibility instead of blaming. Don't live in victim mode. What DOES work is taking responsibility and creating the life you want. Are there things or people that are restricting you, dragging you down, or keeping you busy with things that don't matter? Shed them!

Let go of what no longer serves you. Ask yourself, "Is this helping me to create the life I want for myself?" If not, let it go, and make room for what will take you where you want to go. You don't have to be controlled by other people's guilt, anger, pouting. You don't HAVE to do anything. You can choose what you want to do and how you want to give.

Be compassionate: You don't have to walk on others and forget them in order to move ahead with what you want for your life, but stop rescuing. It's time to allow others to do their own work. That's how they learn and grow. It's true, we all sacrifice at times to help others, but it doesn't have to be you every single time. It is possible to love and give without burning yourself out and becoming sick and resentful.

Swallowed Up

Did you ever have a dream? You may have to go back to your childhood to find it. We all have had dreams at one time or another. Then, as life moves on, the dreams can fade. There are a lot of reasons for this:

You make poor decisions, and no longer believe that you are worthy or capable of going after your dream.

You get caught up in simply surviving and forget how to be creative and proactive about creating the life you want.

You listen to the critics, the nay-sayers, and you begin to believe them. They tell you how crazy you are and how idealistic it is to think you can do what you dreamed of doing.

You become an actor in everyone else's play. It's just easier to stay in the background. It's safer to play small. There's less chance of failing big that way.

You've been disappointed so many times. It's just too much of a risk to hope again.

Why is it even important to have dreams? As human beings, we operate better when we have something to look forward to. It's hard to be hopeful and optimistic if you don't have anything to be hopeful and optimistic about.

We do better when we are intentional. I love the saying, "If you shoot at nothing, you will definitely hit it!" Even if you shoot for something and miss, you did something! At least if you try and fail, you have the opportunity to learn something!

If you are being a martyr and giving up because you won't try or you are getting in your own way, it's time to stop it! You are responsible for creating the life that you want. It may not look exactly like you want when you get there, but it will be a lot better than if you just sit around and blame others and circumstances for letting you down. Remember, you have more power to have what you want than you might think.

Speaking Your Truth

Stuffing doesn't work. It can make you sick. Tired. Invisible. Use your voice to say what needs to be said. Not everything needs to be said, but some things really do. You have a message. What you have to say matters. Speak your truth, and let go of the results.

Experience your feelings. Don't stuff them. Sit with them for a while, but don't let them take over. Feelings are not right or wrong, they just are. Notice them. Practice self-love. Don't dismiss them. They matter. But they are not everything. It's okay if not everyone understands you, or agrees with you, or listens to you. Don't let that stop you from saying what you need to say. Speak up about things you care about.

It's your responsibility to make your boundaries clear and to set consequences for boundary violations. Boundaries that are not made known don't work. Boundaries without consequences don't work. Be clear about your wants and needs. Be clear about what is and isn't okay. Be consistent with your consequences. Then allow others to choose if this works for them. If it doesn't, you may have to re-evaluate the relationship.

It's also okay to ask for help. Sometimes it's just easier to do it yourself. It can feel awkward to be vulnerable and ask others to give up their time and resources for you. But wouldn't you do it for them?

This is good for your humility muscle! You are strong and capable. You could do it by yourself, but sometimes you just need to ask help. It's not a sign of weakness. Ask. Allow others to be a blessing to you just like you have been for so many others.

Most important of all, you have a message, and someone needs to hear it! Stop comparing yourself to others. Stop telling yourself that you don't really have anything valuable to contribute. You are here for a reason. What you have to offer matters. It is profound. It doesn't have to make sense to everyone. It isn't for everyone. It's okay if not everyone gets you or appreciates you, but someone does. God does, and I guarantee there are people that do. They get you. They cherish you. They need you. Don't believe the lie that says, "I don't have anything that anyone wants." It's not true.

Martina McBride's song "Anyway" talks about the fact you never know what your contribution, your story, your song, your love, or your life will mean to others. It can be very disappointing when you feel like you are putting yourself out there and nothing is coming back. But I promise you, it is not in vain. It will touch someone, even if you never hear about it. It doesn't matter what it produces, what matters is that you do your part and share it--because it MATTERS.

Freedom for All

Controlling doesn't work. Remember, it's an illusion! You can only control yourself and what you allow in your life. What works is giving respect, which results in freedom for all. Honor other people's choices, even if they are not the ones you would make. Give what you wish to receive.

Is it really accomplishing what you want if you have to use guilt or manipulation to get someone to do something? That's not empowering! That's bullying and coercion. There's just nothing inspiring about that.

Don't you feel like you operate best when you are truly loved and supported? I'm not talking about when you are in the pleasing zone, where you are just trying to keep all of the balls in the air and people are happy because it is working for them. I mean, when you are making choices that don't hurt others, but ones that work for you. You really are the only one who knows deep down inside what you need to do. It's okay to get input. It's great to ask for feedback. It's necessary to make sure you have a clear perspective. But at the end of the day, you have to make the decisions that will propel you to where you need to go.

Isn't it amazing when you know that you have people in your life that love you no matter what? No matter if you have a bad day or a bad decision. No matter if you do what they think you should. What a gift you give others by doing the same! Loving without strings attached and expectations looming. Everyone living their lives. Loving each other. Making decisions. Celebrating when things go well. Supporting when they don't. This is what we all truly long for. Just the opportunity to love and be loved, period. This is where freedom happens.

> **CONNECTION.**
> SURROUND YOURSELF WITH PEOPLE
> WHO RESPECT AND LIFT YOU UP.
> A SUPPORT GROUP OF PEOPLE WHO
> BELIEVE IN YOU IS NECESSARY.

You take care of your yard; your life. Let others take care of their yard; their life. Stop trespassing where you don't belong. Love. Support. Influence. Inspire. Stop trying to control everything and everyone. You are free to make your choices and live with the consequences, and so is everyone else. What a beautiful thing.

A Day in My Grounded Life

I remind myself that I do have choices.

I do have power.

I do have a lot of say-so in how my day and my life goes.

I reframe.

I readjust.

I remind myself where I've come from, and that it wasn't working.

I get really clear about the fact that I never want to go back to that powerless, boundary-less, non-inspiring place.

I make a different choice; for my day, for my path, and for my future.

Because my days start off better, they also end better. Instead of feeling utterly exhausted and empty, wondering if anything I have done during the day actually made a difference or get my any closer to the life I want, I can lay my head down feeling gratified that I did the best I could with what I had and that is enough.

I also can be satisfied I am living my life with purpose. I am responsible for all that I get done and all that didn't get done. Regardless of whether or not things turn out exactly as I had hoped, there will be another day and another opportunity to make new choices that will take me where I want to go. This is my blessed life; and it can be yours as well.

☐

Chapter 12

Summary

You did it!

Well, here we are! You made it through the foundational steps of boundary-setting. Way to go! This is a huge step, and I hope you can already see the progress you have made and are going to be making soon. It's time to bask in your accomplishments and awareness.

Just because you have finished this book and the first part of the course, it doesn't mean you are an expert! You have come a long way, but this is a lifelong journey. If you continue on the path, you will grow and become more and more aware. Remember that it truly is a journey, and not a destination. You will find that you are mastering some things along the way, and it feels good. You will also notice that depending on where you are at in your life and relationships that new issues may come up and you will feel like you are back at Step 1. This is NORMAL.

You will need to be very intentional as you participate in the on-going process of personal development, self-care, and developing healthy boundaries. Don't get discouraged! Keep doing this "work". You will have setbacks. You will find yourself going back to your old ways if you don't pay attention. You will wonder if you learned anything from this course, but don't give up. Everyone has times like this, but just notice, and get back on track. Sometimes it will feel like you take several steps forward, and then a couple of steps back. It's okay, as long as you keep moving toward healthy emotional well-being.

Highlights

Here is a quick review of some of the major points that we have talked about throughout the book and the course so that you can see how far you've come:

Control

You can't control every circumstance, and you definitely can't control people as much as you would like to sometimes. What you can control is your attitude and your choices, and you can definitely control how much and to whom you will give.

Helping

You can't help everyone and fix everything, and you don't have to. In fact, sometimes you shouldn't. Rescuing and suffering consequences for other people's choices is not helping.

Responsibility

You are responsible for you. Others are responsible for themselves. It is your job to take care of everything within your own "yard".

Honoring

Boundaries is not just about setting them with others, it's about respecting the limits others set even when you don't agree; even when you don't understand. It's about freedom for everyone to make choices and live with the results.

Consequences

Natural consequences are the best teacher for all of us, from children to adults; not nagging, guilt, manipulation, punishment, or anger. The best thing you can do for someone who needs to change is get out of their way and not interrupt the process of making choices and living with the outcome of those choices.

Self-Care

Taking care of yourself is the greatest gift you can give to those around you. It helps you be healthy and happy and able to give more, better, and from a heart full of love and gratitude.

If you have even a small grasp of these principles, you are well on your way to stepping off of that darn perpetual wheel and onto a beautiful path; one that will take you where you want to go in your life.

Stay the course, my friend. I promise it will change your life and your relationships. You can do this. You deserve it!

About Angie Shea

Angie Shea is a Boundaries Coach, Speaker, and an Author. Angie is passionate about helping people create lives and relationships that work by setting healthy limits. She uses her own story, experiences, and breakthroughs to offer hope and solutions to people who are overwhelmed and exhausted. Angie has 2 adult children and resides in Eagle, Idaho.

"Angie's boundaries class has changed mine and my family's life and the way we look at relationships. With our kids, each other and with myself. Her kind and intuitive guidance has been invaluable to my personal growth and I'm forever thankful for her class." —Renee'-

"Angie's course taught me that it's okay to say "no". God does not want me to give all of myself away. The fireman's rule is "You must be safe to save someone else", and I know that in order to help others, I have to take care of myself first." —Shane-

"I have been a part of Angie's classes for about a year and a half now. Through these classes, I have been able to overcome a lot and also set many of my now tried and true boundaries. She shares her own experiences, making it easy to share and grow." —Karen-

Stay Connected

If you resonate with Angie Shea and her work, you can stay connected to her at www.angieshea.com.

Angie is available for:
One-on-one coaching.
Teaching your group.
Speaking at your next event.

Angie also offers Beginning and Advanced Boundaries courses. You can find the latest course schedule on her website.

Contact Angie Shea

You can reach Angie Shea by:
Email: boundariescoaching@gmail.com
Website: www.angieshea.com

Made in the USA
San Bernardino, CA
14 November 2016